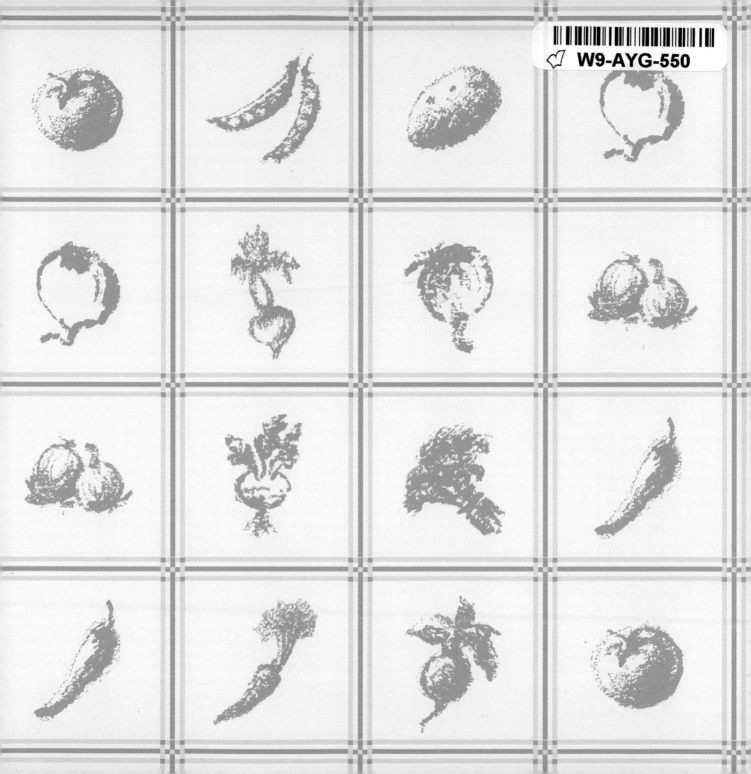

GREETINGS FROM HUNT'S®

The fresh flavor of vine-ripened tomatoes now adds zest to your cooking in new and simple ways, thanks to the Hunt Foods Company's family of fine tomato products.

In *Hunt's Simple Meals for Busy Days* you'll discover 65 exciting recipes that will fit into even the busiest of schedules. Whether you're planning an everyday meal or a special-occasion dinner, these recipes are well-suited to today's on-the-go lifestyle. Choose from the easy skillet dishes, one-dish oven meals, microwave dishes, or crockery cooker meals. Each recipe takes full advantage of tasty, convenient Hunt's tomato products and timesaving cooking techniques.

For more than a century, Hunt's has provided the highest-quality cooking ingredients. We're proud to present our family of tomato products, and we invite you to savor their wonderfully rich and all-natural flavors. With these products on hand, you can be sure of fixing a delicious and wholesome meal in minutes. Enjoy!

CONTENTS

Pictured on the cover: Pronto Italian Chicken (see recipe, page 11).

This seal assures you that every recipe in *Hunt's Simple Meals for Busy Days*
has been tested in the *Better Homes and Gardens*® Test Kitchen. This means
that each recipe is practical and reliable, and meets high standards
of taste appeal.

Produced by Meredith Custom Publishing, 1912 Grand Ave., Des Moines, Iowa 50309-3379.

Hunts®, Homestyle™, Choice-Cut™, and Wesson® are registered trademarks of Hunt-Wesson, Inc.

Making Meals Simple

Hunt's® is proud to present its family of fine tomato products, all ready to add zest and flavor to your favorite meals in minutes.

INSTANT SUCCESS

Hunt's Ready Tomato Sauces offer all the rewards of perfectly seasoned homemade cooking without all the work. These flavorful blends of spices and herbs in a rich, thick tomato sauce make meat, poultry, fish, and pasta dishes a snap to prepare, because Hunt's does the measuring, chopping, and blending for you. Choose from eleven varieties—seven with chunks of firm, vine-ripened tomatoes and four smooth sauces—all with the right combination of spices and seasonings and all-natural ingredients.

FLAVOR AND CONVENIENCE

Hunt's Choice-Cut™ Diced Tomatoes are made from the highest-quality vine-ripened California tomatoes, picked at the peak of the season for optimal flavor and firmness. Because they're already peeled and diced, they're a convenient alternative to whole and fresh tomatoes—perfect for casseroles, soups, and stews, or anytime your recipe calls for tomatoes.

The Finest Ingredients

Call on Hunt's Tomato Paste to add a robust tomato flavor that's perfect for spaghetti sauce, chili, soups, and stews. Available in original and no-salt-added varieties, or with Italian seasonings or garlic already added, Hunt's Tomato Paste is *the* ingredient to use for simmered-to-perfection taste every time.

With its thick texture and its rich tomato flavor, Hunt's Tomato Sauce is a high-quality ingredient to have in your pantry. Keep several cans on hand for casseroles, soups, and one-dish meals. Choose either original or no-salt-added tomato sauce.

Excellent Versatility

Whether you choose Hunt's Whole Tomatoes or Hunt's Stewed Tomatoes, you'll find firm, red California vine-ripened tomatoes that add a wonderfully rich flavor to all your recipes. Hunt's Stewed Tomatoes are masterfully blended with onions, green bell peppers, and celery, and are perfect for soups, sauces and stews. Both products are available with no salt added.

A Family Favorite

For exceptional taste and value, nothing beats Hunt's rich, thick, premium-quality Spaghetti Sauce. Available in nine delicious blends, this 100% natural sauce is ready to heat and serve over your favorite pasta.

Our spaghetti sauces are simmered with vine-ripened tomatoes, sweet onions, and special blends of herbs and spices. For a quick sauce the whole family will love, choose from Hunt's Original, Homestyle™ (no sugar added), Classic Italian, Chunky (with lots of peeled, diced tomatoes), and Light varieties.

SPEEDY SKILLET MEALS

Using just a handful of ingredients, you can create a variety of tempting top-of-the-range recipes in no time at all. Reach for Hunt's® tomato products to whip up new family favorites, including meat and sauce combinations, stir-fries, pasta dishes, and a hearty meatless sensation. Cooking for your family couldn't be easier or more delicious!

Festive Skillet Chicken
(see recipe, page 8)

Festive Skillet Chicken

MAKES 6 TO 8 SERVINGS
PREP TIME: 20 MINUTES • COOK TIME: 40 MINUTES

2½ to 3 pounds meaty chicken pieces
½ cup all-purpose flour
½ teaspoon garlic powder
¼ teaspoon chili powder
2 tablespoons Wesson® Oil
1 14½-ounce can Hunt's® Choice-Cut™ Diced Tomatoes

1 4-ounce can diced green chili peppers, drained
½ cup chopped green pepper
½ cup chopped onion
¼ cup sliced ripe olives
2 tablespoons snipped fresh cilantro
⅛ teaspoon garlic powder
2 to 3 cups hot cooked rice

Rinse chicken; pat dry with paper towels. Combine flour, the ½ teaspoon garlic powder, and the chili powder in a paper or plastic bag. Shake chicken, a few pieces at a time, in flour mixture until well coated. Heat Wesson Oil in a large skillet over medium heat. Cook chicken in the hot oil about 10 minutes or until chicken is lightly browned, turning to brown evenly. Drain off fat.

Meanwhile, combine *undrained* Hunt's Choice-Cut Diced Tomatoes, chili peppers, green pepper, onion, olives, cilantro, and the ⅛ teaspoon garlic powder in a small mixing bowl; mix well. Pour tomato mixture over chicken in skillet. Bring to boiling; reduce heat. Simmer, covered, about 40 minutes or until chicken is tender and no longer pink. Serve over hot cooked rice.

Nutrition facts per serving: 435 cal., 31 g pro., 33 g carbo., 19 g fat, 88 mg chol., 2 g dietary fiber, 508 mg sodium.

Note: Pictured on pages 6–7.

CHICKEN WITH PEPPERS AND TOMATOES

MAKES 6 SERVINGS
TOTAL TIME: 30 MINUTES

6 medium skinless, boneless chicken breast halves	½ cup finely chopped green pepper
⅛ teaspoon black pepper	½ cup finely chopped yellow sweet pepper
1 tablespoon margarine or butter	2 tablespoons dry white wine
1 14½-ounce can Hunt's® Stewed Tomatoes	1 teaspoon chili powder
1 small onion, chopped	¼ teaspoon ground cumin
½ cup finely chopped red sweet pepper	3 cups hot cooked rice

Rinse chicken; pat dry with paper towels. Sprinkle both sides of chicken with black pepper. Melt margarine in a 12-inch skillet. Cook chicken in hot margarine until brown on both sides, turning once. Drain off fat.

Meanwhile, combine *undrained* Hunt's Stewed Tomatoes, onion, red pepper, green pepper, yellow pepper, wine, chili powder, and cumin in a small mixing bowl; mix well.

Pour tomato mixture over chicken in skillet. Bring to boiling; reduce heat. Simmer, covered, for 10 to 12 minutes or until chicken is tender and no longer pink. Remove chicken, using a slotted spoon. Arrange chicken on a serving platter; keep chicken warm.

Heat the tomato mixture over medium heat to boiling. Boil, uncovered, for 6 to 8 minutes or until desired consistency. Spoon tomato mixture over chicken on serving platter. Serve with hot cooked rice.

Nutrition facts per serving: 289 cal., 23 g pro., 34 g carbo., 5 g fat, 54 mg chol., 1 g dietary fiber, 184 mg sodium.

CHICKEN MARENGO

MAKES 4 SERVINGS
PREP TIME: 15 MINUTES • COOK TIME: 15 MINUTES

4   medium skinless, boneless chicken
     breast halves
½   small onion, sliced
½   teaspoon bottled minced garlic
2   cups sliced fresh mushrooms

1   15-ounce can Hunt's® Ready Tomato
     Sauces Original Italian
1   2¼-ounce can sliced ripe olives,
     drained

Coat and brown chicken as directed in tip on *opposite page*; remove and set aside. Add onion and garlic to skillet; cook and stir for 1 minute. Add mushrooms; cook and stir until tender. Drain off fat. Stir in Hunt's Ready Tomato Sauces Original Italian and olives. Return chicken to skillet; spoon sauce over. Bring to boil; reduce heat. Simmer, covered, about 15 minutes or until chicken is tender and no longer pink.

Nutrition facts per serving: 185 cal., 23 g pro., 12 g carbo., 5 g fat, 54 mg chol., 4 g dietary fiber, 598 mg sodium.

CHICKEN MARSALA

MAKES 4 SERVINGS
PREP TIME: 15 MINUTES • COOK TIME: 15 MINUTES

4   medium skinless, boneless chicken
     breast halves
3   cups sliced fresh mushrooms
1   cup sliced onion
½   teaspoon bottled minced garlic

1   15-ounce can Hunt's® Ready Tomato
     Sauces Chunky Special
⅓   cup Marsala wine
¼   teaspoon sugar

Coat and brown chicken as directed in tip on *opposite page*; remove and set aside. Add mushrooms, onion, and garlic to skillet; cook and stir until tender. Drain off fat. Stir in Hunt's Ready Tomato Sauces Chunky Special, Marsala wine, and sugar. Return chicken to skillet; spoon sauce over. Bring to boiling; reduce heat. Simmer, covered, about 15 minutes or until chicken is tender and no longer pink.

Nutrition facts per serving: 185 cal., 23 g pro., 13 g carbo., 4 g fat, 54 mg chol., 3 g dietary fiber, 293 mg sodium.

PRONTO ITALIAN CHICKEN

MAKES 4 SERVINGS
PREP TIME: 20 MINUTES • COOK TIME: 15 MINUTES

- 4 medium skinless, boneless chicken breast halves
- 2 cups sliced fresh mushrooms
- 1 cup chopped onion
- 1 small zucchini, thinly sliced
- 1 15-ounce can Hunt's® Ready Tomato Sauces Chunky Garlic and Herb
- 2 tablespoons dry white wine

Coat and brown chicken as directed in tip *below*; remove and set aside. Add mushrooms, onion, and zucchini to skillet; cook and stir until tender. Drain off fat. Stir in Hunt's Ready Tomato Sauces Chunky Garlic and Herb and wine. Return chicken to skillet; spoon sauce over. Bring to boiling; reduce heat. Simmer, covered, about 15 minutes or until chicken is tender and no longer pink.

Nutrition facts per serving: 204 cal., 23 g pro., 18 g carbo., 3 g fat, 54 mg chol., 3 g dietary fiber, 374 mg sodium.

Note: Pictured on cover.

BROWNING CHICKEN

When you follow these easy steps, you can count on moist, perfectly browned chicken every time.

Rinse the chicken pieces; pat dry with paper towels. Sprinkle the chicken with salt and pepper. Place all-purpose flour in a shallow dish; coat the chicken lightly with flour on all sides.

Heat Wesson® Oil in a large skillet (use 2 tablespoons oil for 4 chicken breast halves). Add the chicken pieces and cook over medium heat, turning frequently, about 10 minutes or until golden brown on all sides.

Savory Turkey over Spaghetti Squash

MAKES 4 SERVINGS
TOTAL TIME: 30 MINUTES

1 3- to 4-pound spaghetti squash, quartered	2 cups Hunt's® Original Traditional Spaghetti Sauce*
1 pound ground fresh turkey	¼ teaspoon seasoned salt
1 teaspoon bottled minced garlic	¼ teaspoon pepper
	Grated Parmesan or Romano cheese

Place squash pieces in a 4½-quart Dutch oven; add water to a depth of 2 inches. Bring to boiling; reduce heat. Simmer, partially covered, about 20 minutes or until squash strands separate from rind.

Meanwhile, cook ground turkey and garlic in a 10-inch skillet about 3 minutes or until turkey no longer is pink. Drain off fat. Stir Hunt's Original Traditional Spaghetti Sauce, seasoned salt, and pepper into turkey mixture; cook about 2 minutes more or until heated through.

Use tongs to remove squash from Dutch oven; drain. Use 2 forks to remove strands of squash from rind; pile squash strands on a serving platter. Spoon turkey and sauce mixture over squash; sprinkle with grated cheese. Serve immediately.

*Note: Store the leftover spaghetti sauce in a tightly covered plastic container in the refrigerator for up to 1 week.

Nutrition facts per serving: 334 cal., 26 g pro., 22 g carbo., 16 g fat, 68 mg chol., 8 g dietary fiber, 838 mg sodium.

TASTE TWIST ON PIZZA

Rich, all-purpose Hunt's® Spaghetti Sauce adds a unique flavor to homemade pizza. Spread some sauce on a homemade or purchased pizza crust. Then, add your favorite toppers and bake for a pizzeria-fresh treat.

 Fajita Pitas

MAKES 6 SERVINGS
TOTAL TIME: 15 MINUTES

1¼ pounds skinless, boneless chicken breast halves
2 tablespoons Wesson® Oil
1 large green pepper, sliced
1 medium onion, sliced
1 15-ounce can Hunt's® Ready Tomato Sauces Chunky Salsa
6 pita bread, halved crosswise

Rinse chicken; pat dry with paper towels. Cut chicken into bite-size strips. Heat Wesson Oil in a large skillet. Stir-fry chicken strips, green pepper, and onion in hot oil until chicken is tender and no longer pink. Drain off fat.

Stir Hunt's Ready Tomato Sauces Chunky Salsa into chicken mixture; cook over medium heat until heated through. Spoon chicken mixture into pita bread halves. Serve immediately.

Nutrition facts per serving: 363 cal., 29 g pro., 41 g carbo., 8 g fat, 60 mg chol., 3 g dietary fiber, 748 mg sodium.

QUICK READY SAUCES FIX-UPS

Hunt's® Ready Tomato Sauces are the perfect partners for broiled or grilled meats such as chicken breasts, pork chops, fish steaks, and burgers. They also make winning toppers for egg dishes or baked potatoes. For variety, choose from any of Hunt's seven Chunky Ready Sauces such as Italian, Garlic and Herb, or Salsa or one of Hunt's smooth Ready Sauces such as the Original Italian flavor.

CHICKEN PAPRIKA

MAKES 4 SERVINGS
TOTAL TIME: 30 MINUTES

¼ cup margarine or butter	2 cups cubed cooked chicken (10 ounces)
3 cups sliced fresh mushrooms	
1 medium onion, chopped	1 14½-ounce can chicken broth
2 cloves garlic, minced	2 tablespoons Hunt's® Tomato Paste
2 to 3 teaspoons Hungarian paprika or paprika	1 8-ounce carton dairy sour cream
	3 tablespoons all-purpose flour
¼ teaspoon pepper	½ pound packaged dried wide noodles, cooked and drained

Melt margarine or butter in a 10-inch skillet over medium heat. Cook and stir mushrooms, onion, and garlic in melted margarine or butter about 5 minutes or until vegetables are tender. Stir in paprika and pepper. Cook and stir 1 minute more. Stir in cubed cooked chicken, chicken broth, and Hunt's Tomato Paste. Bring to boiling.

Stir together sour cream and flour; stir into mixture in skillet. Cook and stir until thickened and bubbly. Cook and stir 1 minute more. Serve chicken mixture over cooked noodles.

Nutrition facts per serving: 634 cal., 37 g pro., 55 g carbo., 31 g fat, 175 mg chol., 2 g dietary fiber, 678 mg sodium.

BEEF STROGANOFF

MAKES 4 SERVINGS
TOTAL TIME: 20 MINUTES

¾ **pound boneless beef sirloin steak, cut
½ to ¾ inch thick and partially
frozen**
1 **8-ounce carton dairy sour cream**
2 **tablespoons all-purpose flour**
1 **tablespoon Hunt's® Tomato Paste**
½ **cup cold water**
1 **teaspoon instant beef bouillon granules**

⅛ **teaspoon pepper
Wesson® No Stick Cooking Spray**
2 **cups sliced fresh mushrooms**
1 **medium onion, chopped**
1 **clove garlic, minced**
½ **pound packaged dried fettuccine,
cooked and drained**
1 **tablespoon snipped parsley**

Trim fat from beef; thinly slice meat across the grain into bite-size strips and set aside.

Stir together sour cream, flour, and Hunt's Tomato Paste in a small mixing bowl. Stir in cold water, beef bouillon granules, and pepper. Set aside.

Spray a *cold* large skillet with Wesson No Stick Cooking Spray. Heat the skillet over medium heat. Add beef to the hot skillet. Stir-fry for 2 to 3 minutes or until desired doneness. Remove beef from the skillet; set aside. Add mushrooms, onion, and garlic. Stir-fry for 3 to 4 minutes or until the vegetables are tender.

Add the sour cream mixture to the skillet; cook and stir over medium heat until thickened and bubbly. Return meat to the skillet; cook and stir about 2 minutes more or until heated through. Serve meat mixture over hot cooked fettuccine. Sprinkle with snipped parsley.

*Nutrition facts per serving: 499 cal., 31 g pro., 52 g carbo.,
19 g fat, 94 mg chol., 2 g dietary fiber, 320 mg sodium.*

 Beef Strips with Pasta

MAKES 4 SERVINGS
TOTAL TIME: 20 MINUTES

½ pound boneless beef top round steak, partially frozen

½ pound packaged dried vermicelli or spaghetti

1 9-ounce package frozen Italian-style green beans or cut green beans

1 tablespoon Wesson® Oil

1 medium onion, chopped

1 14½-ounce can Hunt's® Choice-Cut™ Diced Tomatoes

1 4-ounce can sliced mushrooms, drained

½ of a 6-ounce can (⅓ cup) Hunt's Tomato Paste

½ teaspoon fennel seed, crushed (optional)

¼ teaspoon pepper

2 tablespoons grated Parmesan cheese

Trim fat from meat; thinly slice meat across the grain into bite-size strips.

Cook pasta according to package directions, adding frozen green beans to the pasta for the last 5 minutes of cooking. Drain; keep warm.

Meanwhile, for sauce, heat Wesson Oil in a large skillet over medium-high heat. Add meat and onion. Stir-fry for 2 to 3 minutes or until meat is brown. Drain off fat.

Stir in *undrained* Hunt's Choice-Cut Diced Tomatoes, the mushrooms, Hunt's Tomato Paste, fennel seed (if desired), and pepper. Bring to boiling; reduce heat. Simmer, covered, about 5 minutes or until heated through, stirring occasionally.

Arrange pasta mixture on individual plates or a large platter. Spoon the sauce over the pasta mixture. Sprinkle with Parmesan cheese.

Nutrition facts per serving: 395 cal., 31 g pro., 57 g carbo., 8 g fat, 38 mg chol., 4 g dietary fiber, 478 mg sodium.

$\mathcal{S}$WIFT SWISS STEAK

MAKES 6 SERVINGS
PREP TIME: 20 MINUTES • COOK TIME: 30 MINUTES

2 tablespoons all-purpose flour
½ teaspoon onion salt
¼ to ½ teaspoon black pepper
6 beef cubed steaks (about 1½ pounds total)
4 teaspoons Wesson® Oil
1 14½-ounce can Hunt's® Stewed Tomatoes

1 8-ounce can Hunt's Tomato Sauce
½ teaspoon dried savory or marjoram, crushed
1 medium green pepper, cut into strips
¾ pound packaged dried noodles, cooked and drained

Stir together flour, onion salt, and black pepper in a shallow dish. Dip cubed steaks into flour mixture, coating both sides. Heat Wesson Oil in a large skillet over medium heat. Cook steaks, *half* at a time, in hot oil until brown on both sides. Drain off fat. Return all meat to skillet.

Add *undrained* Hunt's Stewed Tomatoes, Hunt's Tomato Sauce, and savory to skillet. Bring to boiling; reduce heat. Simmer, covered, for 25 minutes, stirring occasionally. Add green pepper; cover and simmer for 5 to 7 minutes more or until steaks are done and green pepper is tender.

Transfer steaks to a serving platter, reserving juices; keep warm. Skim fat from juices; pour juices over meat. Serve meat with hot cooked noodles.

Nutrition facts per serving: 394 cal., 31 g pro., 39 g carbo., 12 g fat, 110 mg chol., 4 g dietary fiber, 619 mg sodium.

CHILI MACARONI

MAKES 4 SERVINGS
PREP TIME: 15 MINUTES • COOK TIME: 15 MINUTES

¾ pound ground beef or ground fresh turkey
1 medium onion, chopped
1 14½-ounce can Hunt's® Choice-Cut™ Diced Tomatoes
1¼ cups Hunt's Tomato Juice
1 4-ounce can diced green chili peppers, drained

2 teaspoons chili powder
½ teaspoon garlic salt
1 cup packaged dried wagon-wheel macaroni or elbow macaroni
1 cup loose-pack frozen cut green beans
1 cup shredded cheddar cheese (4 ounces)

Cook ground beef or turkey and onion in a large skillet until meat is brown. Drain off fat. Stir *undrained* Hunt's Choice-Cut Diced Tomatoes, Hunt's Tomato Juice, chili peppers, chili powder, and garlic salt into meat mixture. Bring to boiling. Stir in *uncooked* macaroni and green beans. Return to boiling; reduce heat. Simmer, covered, about 15 minutes or until macaroni and beans are tender. To serve, spoon into bowls; sprinkle with cheese.

Nutrition facts per serving: 460 cal., 32 g pro., 34 g carbo., 22 g fat, 93 mg chol., 3 g dietary fiber, 1,211 mg sodium.

NEW CHOICES FOR PIZZA LOVERS

Liven up the flavor of pizza by using one of the Hunt's® Ready Tomato Sauces in place of pizza sauce. (One 15-ounce can contains enough sauce for two large pizzas.) To make a tasty taco pizza, for instance, spread your favorite homemade or purchased pizza crusts with the Chunky Salsa flavor of Hunt's Ready Tomato Sauces. Spoon on refried beans, then sprinkle on cooked ground beef or sausage and shredded cheese. Bake as directed in the crust recipe or on the package. Top the finished pizza with shredded lettuce and crushed tortilla chips for a tempting south-of-the-border taste.

$\mathcal{V}$EAL PAPRIKA

MAKES 4 SERVINGS
TOTAL TIME: 35 MINUTES

1 pound boneless veal leg round steak, partially frozen	1 teaspoon instant beef bouillon granules
1 tablespoon Wesson® Oil	½ teaspoon dried basil, crushed
1 cup sliced fresh mushrooms	½ teaspoon salt
1 medium onion, thinly sliced	¼ teaspoon pepper
1 clove garlic, minced	1 8-ounce carton dairy sour cream
1 8-ounce can Hunt's® Tomato Sauce	2 tablespoons all-purpose flour
½ cup water	½ pound packaged dried noodles, cooked and drained
2 teaspoons paprika	2 tablespoons snipped parsley

Thinly slice veal across the grain into bite-size strips. Heat Wesson Oil in a large skillet over medium-high heat. Cook and stir *half* of the veal in hot oil for 2 to 3 minutes or until brown. Remove veal from skillet; repeat with remaining veal. Remove all veal from skillet; set aside.

Add mushrooms, onion, and garlic to skillet; cook and stir for 3 to 4 minutes or until vegetables are tender. Drain off fat. Stir Hunt's Tomato Sauce, water, paprika, beef bouillon granules, basil, salt, and pepper into vegetable mixture. Bring to boiling. Stir together sour cream and flour; add to skillet. Cook and stir until thickened and bubbly. Cook and stir 1 minute more. Return meat to skillet. Cook and stir until heated through. Serve over hot cooked noodles. Sprinkle each serving with parsley.

Nutrition facts per serving: 531 cal., 34 g pro., 52 g carbo., 21 g fat, 192 mg chol., 2 g dietary fiber, 937 mg sodium.

CURRIED PORK CHOPS

MAKES 4 SERVINGS
PREP TIME: 20 MINUTES • COOK TIME: 10 MINUTES

3 tablespoons all-purpose flour
  Seasoned salt
  Ground black pepper
4 pork loin chops, cut ¾ inch thick
  (about 1½ pounds total)
2 tablespoons Wesson® Oil
1 medium onion, cut into eighths

1 medium apple, cored and cut
  into eighths
1 15-ounce can Hunt's® Ready Tomato
  Sauces Chunky Special
¼ cup raisins
2 teaspoons curry powder
1 teaspoon sugar
⅛ teaspoon ground red pepper

Stir together flour, seasoned salt, and black pepper in a shallow dish. Dip pork chops into flour mixture, coating both sides. Heat Wesson Oil in large skillet. Cook and stir onion and apple in hot oil until onion is tender. Remove from skillet; set aside. Cook chops in hot skillet until lightly brown on both sides. Remove chops from skillet. Drain off fat. Stir Hunt's Ready Tomato Sauces Chunky Special, raisins, curry powder, sugar, and ground red pepper into skillet. Return chops, apple, and onion to skillet. Bring to boiling; reduce heat. Simmer, covered, 10 to 15 minutes or until pork chops are tender and no longer pink.

Nutrition facts per serving: 333 cal., 21 g pro., 28 g carbo.,
16 g fat, 58 mg chol., 4 g dietary fiber, 302 mg sodium.

PERFECT PASTA SALAD TO GO

For summer celebrations, marinate a potluck-size salad with Hunt's® Choice-Cut™ Diced Tomatoes. Toss together ¾ pound *rotini* or *large elbow macaroni*, cooked and drained; 1 cup chopped *green pepper*; 3 cups cut-up *fresh vegetables*; and ½ cup sliced pitted *ripe olives*. Stir in one 14½-ounce can *Hunt's Choice-Cut Diced Tomatoes* and ¾ cup bottled *Italian salad dressing*. Cover and chill in the refrigerator for 4 to 24 hours. Serves 10 to 12.

FISH CREOLE

MAKES 4 SERVINGS
TOTAL TIME: 35 MINUTES

1 pound fresh or frozen swordfish, sea bass, or tuna steaks, cut 1 inch thick	1 tablespoon Wesson® Oil
1 14½-ounce can Hunt's® Whole Tomatoes, cut up	1 medium onion, chopped
½ teaspoon salt	1 stalk celery, thinly sliced
½ teaspoon sugar	1 medium green pepper, cut into 2-inch strips
⅛ to ¼ teaspoon ground red pepper	2 tablespoons snipped parsley
	2 cups hot cooked rice

Thaw fish steaks, if frozen. Rinse fish; pat dry with paper towels. Cut fish into 1-inch cubes; set aside. Stir together *undrained* Hunt's Whole Tomatoes (cut up), salt, sugar, and ground red pepper in a small bowl; set aside.

Heat Wesson Oil in large skillet or wok over medium-high heat. (Add more Wesson Oil as necessary during cooking.) Stir-fry onion and celery in hot oil for 2 minutes. Add green pepper; stir-fry about 2 minutes more or until vegetables are crisp-tender. Remove vegetables from the skillet or wok.

Add *half* of the fish to the hot skillet or wok. Stir-fry for 3 to 6 minutes or until fish flakes easily when tested with a fork, being careful not to break up pieces. Remove fish from the skillet or wok. Repeat with remaining fish. Drain off fat. Remove all of the fish from the skillet or wok; set aside.

Stir tomato mixture; add to the hot skillet or wok. Return cooked vegetables to the skillet or wok, stirring to combine. Cook and stir about 3 minutes or until slightly thickened. Add parsley. Gently stir in cooked fish; cook for 1 to 2 minutes more or until heated through. Serve immediately in bowls over hot cooked rice.

Nutrition facts per serving: 330 cal., 26 g pro., 37 g carbo., 8 g fat, 43 mg chol., 2 g dietary fiber, 658 mg sodium.

CORNMEAL-COATED FILLETS

MAKES 6 SERVINGS
TOTAL TIME: 25 MINUTES

1½ pounds fresh or frozen skinless perch or catfish fillets, cut ½ inch thick
⅓ cup all-purpose flour
2 tablespoons cornmeal
1 teaspoon garlic salt
1 teaspoon chili powder

½ teaspoon ground red pepper
½ teaspoon paprika
2 tablespoons margarine or butter
2 tablespoons Wesson® Oil
1 15-ounce can Hunt's® Ready Tomato Sauces Chunky Special

Thaw fish, if frozen. Rinse fish; pat dry with paper towels. Stir together flour, cornmeal, garlic salt, chili powder, ground red pepper, and paprika in a shallow dish. Dip fish fillets into flour mixture, coating both sides.

Heat *half* of the margarine and *half* of the Wesson Oil in a large skillet over medium heat. Add *half* of the fish to skillet in a single layer. Fry for 3 to 4 minutes on each side or until golden and crisp and the fish flakes easily when tested with a fork. Remove from skillet; drain on paper towels. Repeat with remaining margarine, Wesson Oil, and fish.

Meanwhile, place Hunt's Ready Tomato Sauces Chunky Special in a medium saucepan. Cook, stirring often, until heated through. Serve over fish.

Nutrition facts per serving: 242 cal., 23 g pro., 13 g carbo., 11 g fat, 48 mg chol., 2 g dietary fiber, 565 mg sodium.

SPICY SHRIMP PASTA SAUCE

MAKES 4 SERVINGS
TOTAL TIME: 30 MINUTES

1 pound fresh or frozen shrimp
  in the shells*
1 tablespoon olive oil
1 medium onion, sliced
2 teaspoons bottled minced garlic

2 15-ounce cans Hunt's® Ready Tomato
  Sauces Chunky Italian
⅛ teaspoon crushed red pepper
½ pound packaged dried spaghetti
  or fettuccine, cooked and drained

Thaw shrimp, if frozen. Peel and devein shrimp; set aside. Heat oil in a large skillet. Cook and stir onion and garlic in hot oil until onion is tender. Add shrimp; cook and stir until shrimp turn pink. Drain off fat. Stir in Hunt's Ready Tomato Sauces Chunky Italian and crushed red pepper; heat through. Serve over hot cooked spaghetti or fettuccine.

Note: Substitute ½ pound peeled cooked shrimp, if you like. Because this shrimp is already cooked, add it to the skillet at the same time you add the Hunt's Ready Tomato Sauces.

Nutrition facts per serving: 348 cal., 19 g pro., 54 g carbo.,
7 g fat, 83 mg chol., 3 g dietary fiber, 595 mg sodium.

PARTY PERFECT IDEAS

For quick and easy entertaining, keep several cans of Hunt's® Ready Tomato Sauces on hand, and you'll have instant appetizers your guests will love. Hunt's Ready Tomato Sauces Chunky Salsa is perfect for serving with nachos, quesadillas, or tortilla chips. And the Chunky Garlic and Herb blend makes an excellent dipping sauce for chilled cooked shrimp.

Hearty Rice Skillet

Makes 4 Servings
Total Time: 30 Minutes

1 15-ounce can black beans, garbanzo beans, or kidney beans, rinsed and drained	½ teaspoon dried thyme or dillweed, crushed
1 14½-ounce can Hunt's® Stewed Tomatoes	Several dashes bottled hot pepper sauce (optional)
2 cups loose-pack frozen mixed vegetables	1 8-ounce can Hunt's Tomato Sauce
1 cup water	⅓ cup slivered almonds, toasted
¾ cup quick-cooking brown rice	½ cup shredded mozzarella or cheddar cheese (2 ounces)

Combine beans, *undrained* Hunt's Stewed Tomatoes, frozen mixed vegetables, water, *uncooked* rice, and thyme in a large skillet. Stir in hot pepper sauce, if desired. Bring to boiling; reduce heat. Simmer, covered, for 12 to 14 minutes or until rice is tender. Stir in Hunt's Tomato Sauce; heat through.

To serve, stir in toasted almonds. Sprinkle with shredded mozzarella or cheddar cheese.

Nutrition facts per serving: 399 cal., 20 g pro., 65 g carbo., 10 g fat, 8 mg chol., 8 g dietary fiber, 1,028 mg sodium.

Toasting Almonds

Spend just a few minutes toasting almonds and you can enjoy their rich, nutty flavor in dishes such as Hearty Rice Skillet *above*. Spread the nuts in a thin layer in a shallow baking pan. Bake in a 350° oven, stirring once or twice, for 5 to 10 minutes or until the almonds are golden.

EXTRA-EASY OVEN MEALS

In just a short time, you can have a delicious meal ready for the oven. Prepare these one-dish wonders—all featuring the fabulous flavors of Hunt's® tomato products. For added convenience, most of these recipes feature vegetable, pasta, or rice accompaniments that bake right along with the meat.

Tamale Pie
(see recipe, page 32)

TAMALE PIE

MAKES 6 SERVINGS
PREP TIME: 45 MINUTES • CHILL TIME: I HOUR
COOK TIME: 30 MINUTES

1½ cups cold water	½ cup chopped carrot
½ cup yellow cornmeal	1 clove garlic, minced
¼ teaspoon salt	2 teaspoons chili powder
¼ teaspoon ground cumin	1 15-ounce can Hunt's® Tomato Sauce
⅛ teaspoon black pepper	1 12-ounce can whole kernel corn, drained
2 teaspoons margarine or butter	1 4-ounce can diced green chili peppers, drained
1 pound ground beef	
1 cup chopped onion	½ cup sliced pitted ripe olives
1 cup chopped green or red sweet pepper	

Combine cold water, cornmeal, salt, cumin, and black pepper in a small saucepan. Bring just to boiling; reduce heat. Stir in margarine or butter; cook over low heat for 10 minutes, stirring often. Remove from heat. Spread mixture on waxed paper into an 8-inch square. Chill about 1 hour or until set.

Cook ground beef, onion, green or red sweet pepper, carrot, garlic, and chili powder in a large skillet until meat is brown and onion is tender. Drain off fat. Stir in Hunt's Tomato Sauce, corn, chili peppers, and olives. Cook and stir until bubbly. Spoon mixture into a 2-quart rectangular baking dish.

Cut cornmeal mixture into diamond shapes. Place shapes on top of meat mixture. Bake in a 350° oven for 30 to 40 minutes or until heated through.

Nutrition facts per serving: 323 cal., 21 g pro., 30 g carbo., 14 g fat, 56 mg chol., 5 g dietary fiber, 1,061 mg sodium.

Note: Pictured on pages 30–31.

Broiled Chicken Salad With Salsa Dressing

Makes 4 Servings
Prep Time: 15 Minutes • Cook Time: 8 Minutes

4 medium skinless, boneless chicken
   breast halves
   Salsa Dressing (see recipe, *below*)
6 cups torn mixed greens

2 cups assorted salad ingredients cut
   into bite-size pieces (cucumber,
   green pepper, celery carrot,
   and/or red cabbage)

Rinse chicken. Place chicken in a medium mixing bowl. Pour *1 cup* of the Salsa Dressing over chicken breasts; stir to coat chicken well. Cover; refrigerate chicken to marinate for 8 to 24 hours.

Drain chicken, discarding marinade. Place chicken on unheated rack of broiler pan. Broil chicken 3 inches from heat for 4 to 5 minutes on each side or until chicken is tender and no longer pink. Arrange greens and salad ingredients on 4 individual salad plates. Slice cooked chicken into thin strips and arrange on top of salads. Spoon some of the remaining Salsa Dressing over each serving.

Salsa Dressing: Stir together one 15-ounce can *Hunt's® Ready Tomato Sauces Chunky Salsa* and 1 cup prepared or bottled *Italian salad dressing* in medium mixing bowl. Store in tightly covered container in the refrigerator for up to 1 week.

Nutrition facts per serving: 347 cal., 23 g pro., 14 g carbo., 22 g fat, 54 mg chol., 3 g dietary fiber, 754 mg sodium.

Add Spice with Salsa Dressing

Use the leftover Salsa Dressing created with Hunt's® Ready Tomato Sauces Chunky Salsa in the recipe *above* to liven up the flavors of other salads, too. Drizzle it on chef's salad, spoon it over taco salad, or toss it into pasta salad for an irresistible, tangy sensation.

CHILI CHICKEN AND BROWN RICE

MAKES 6 SERVINGS
PREP TIME: 25 MINUTES • COOK TIME: 30 MINUTES

6	medium skinless, boneless chicken breast halves or 1 pound turkey breast tenderloin steaks, cut into 6 portions
1	tablespoon Wesson® Oil
1	medium onion, chopped
½	cup chopped green, yellow, and/or red sweet pepper
1	clove garlic, minced
1	14½-ounce can Hunt's® Stewed Tomatoes

1	14½-ounce can chicken broth
1¾	cups quick-cooking or instant brown rice
	Several dashes bottled hot pepper sauce
½	cup shredded cheddar or Monterey Jack cheese (2 ounces)
6	pitted ripe olives, sliced
¾	cup plain yogurt

Rinse chicken or turkey; pat dry with paper towels. Heat Wesson Oil in a large skillet. Cook chicken or turkey in hot oil about 2 minutes on each side or until brown. Remove from skillet; set aside. Add onion, sweet pepper, and garlic to the skillet; cook and stir until vegetables are tender. Drain off fat. Stir in *undrained* Hunt's Stewed Tomatoes, chicken broth, *uncooked* brown rice, and hot pepper sauce. Bring to boiling. Spoon mixture into a 2-quart rectangular baking dish. Arrange chicken or turkey on top of the rice mixture.

Bake, covered, in a 350° oven for 30 to 35 minutes or until rice is tender. Uncover; sprinkle with shredded cheddar or Monterey Jack cheese. Let stand about 5 minutes or until cheese is melted. Sprinkle with olives; top with yogurt.

Nutrition facts per serving: 411 cal., 27 g pro., 49 g carbo., 11 g fat, 60 mg chol., 3 g dietary fiber, 657 mg sodium.

Savory Oven Beef Stew

MAKES 4 TO 6 SERVINGS
PREP TIME: 15 MINUTES • COOK TIME: 2 HOURS

2 tablespoons Wesson® Oil	2 medium potatoes, sliced ½ inch thick
1 pound beef stew meat, cut into 1-inch cubes	2 small onions, cut into wedges
1 15-ounce can Hunt's® Ready Tomato Sauces Chunky Italian	2 small carrots, sliced
1 14½-ounce can Hunt's Choice-Cut™ Diced Tomatoes	1 small green pepper, cut into strips
	1 cup sliced celery

Heat Wesson Oil in a large skillet. Cook stew meat, *half* at a time, in hot oil until brown, stirring occasionally. Drain off fat. Return all meat to the skillet. Stir in Hunt's Ready Tomato Sauces Chunky Italian and *undrained* Hunt's Choice-Cut Diced Tomatoes; cook and stir until bubbly. Spoon into a 3-quart casserole. Stir in potatoes, onions, carrots, green pepper, and celery. Bake, covered, in a 350° oven for 2 to 2¼ hours or until meat and vegetables are tender, stirring occasionally. Skim off fat before serving.

Nutrition facts per serving: 422 cal., 31 g pro., 33 g carbo., 19 g fat, 86 mg chol., 7 g dietary fiber, 1,041 mg sodium.

HANDY DICED TOMATOES

Punch up your cooking—pronto—by keeping plenty of Hunt's® Choice-Cut™ Diced Tomatoes on hand. For a tasty vegetable dish, combine cooked corn or lima beans with the tomatoes and heat through. Or, give your homemade vegetable or bean soup a flavor boost by adding diced tomatoes.

Whenever a recipe calls for cutting up canned tomatoes, substitute diced tomatoes. You'll trim the prep time but keep the full, rich taste.

PORK AND GREEN CHILI CASSEROLE

MAKES 8 SERVINGS
PREP TIME: 35 MINUTES • COOK TIME: 35 MINUTES

1 tablespoon **Wesson®** Oil	2 4-ounce cans diced green chili
1½ pounds boneless pork shoulder roast,	peppers, drained
cut into bite-size pieces	½ cup Hunt's Ready Tomato Sauces
2 cups quick-cooking brown rice	Chunky Salsa*
1 15-ounce can black beans, rinsed	1 teaspoon garlic powder
and drained	1 teaspoon ground cumin
1 14½-ounce can Hunt's® Choice-Cut™	½ teaspoon black pepper
Diced Tomatoes	2 cups shredded cheddar cheese
1 10¾-ounce can condensed cream	(8 ounces)
of chicken soup	

Heat Wesson Oil in a 12-inch skillet over medium-high heat. Stir-fry pork, *half* at a time, in hot oil until no longer pink. Drain off fat. Return all meat to skillet. Stir in *uncooked* rice, black beans, *undrained* Hunt's Choice-Cut Diced Tomatoes, condensed soup, chili peppers, Hunt's Ready Tomato Sauces Chunky Salsa, garlic powder, cumin, and black pepper. Cook, stirring often, until bubbly; pour into 3-quart rectangular baking dish. Bake, covered, in a 375° oven about 30 minutes or until rice is tender. Uncover; sprinkle with cheese. Bake, uncovered, 4 to 5 minutes more or until cheese melts.

*Note: Store leftover chunky salsa sauce in a tightly covered plastic container in refrigerator for up to 1 week. See tips on pages 14, 21, 27, and 66 for ideas on how to use the sauce.

Nutrition facts per serving: 530 cal., 34 g pro., 51 g carbo., 22 g fat, 98 mg chol., 3 g dietary fiber, 1,210 mg sodium.

THE PERFECT ACCOMPANIMENT

Succulent side dishes are a snap when you call on Hunt's® tomato products. Simply follow package directions to prepare brown or long-grain rice, couscous, or pasta. Then, stir in your favorite Hunt's Spaghetti Sauce and heat.

Hearty Combo Pizza

Makes 6 to 8 Servings
Prep Time: 45 Minutes • Cook Time: 10 Minutes

Homemade Pizza Crusts (see tip, page 40) or two 12-inch purchased pizza crusts
½ pound ground beef and/or bulk Italian sausage or pork sausage
1 cup chopped onion
1 15-ounce can Hunt's® Ready Tomato Sauces Chunky Garlic and Herb

1 3½-ounce package sliced pepperoni
1 cup cut-up Canadian-style bacon
1 cup chopped green pepper
2 cups shredded mozzarella cheese (8 ounces)
¼ cup grated Parmesan or Romano cheese

Grease two 12-inch pizza pans or two large baking sheets. On a lightly floured surface, roll each half of the Homemade Pizza Crusts dough into a 13-inch circle; transfer to pans. (If using purchased crusts, follow package directions.) Build up edges; flute. Prick dough well with a fork. Do not let rise. Bake in a 425° oven for 10 to 12 minutes or until golden.

Meanwhile, cook meat and onion in a large skillet until meat is brown. Drain off fat. Spread Hunt's Ready Tomato Sauces Chunky Garlic and Herb over hot crusts. Sprinkle with meat mixture. Top with pepperoni, Canadian-style bacon, and green pepper. Sprinkle with cheeses.

Bake pizzas for 10 to 12 minutes more or until cheeses melt and sauce is bubbly.

Nutrition facts per serving: 629 cal., 36 g pro., 57 g carbo., 27 g fat, 80 mg chol., 4 g dietary fiber, 1,280 mg sodium.

Freeze Now, Serve Later

For an easy make-ahead meal, freeze one of the unbaked pizzas from the recipe *above* or on *page 40*. (Be sure to wrap it in foil or freezer wrap first.) When you're ready to serve it, unwrap the frozen pizza and place it on a baking sheet. Bake, uncovered, in a 425° oven for 20 to 25 minutes or until heated through.

CHEESEBURGER PIZZA

MAKES 8 SERVINGS
PREP TIME: 20 MINUTES • COOK TIME: 12 MINUTES

2 12-inch purchased pizza crusts
   or Homemade Pizza Crusts
   (see tip, *below*)
1 pound ground beef
1 cup chopped onion
1 15-ounce can Hunt's® Ready Tomato
   Sauces Chunky Italian

1 14½-ounce can Hunt's® Choice-Cut™
   Diced Tomatoes, drained
6 slices bacon, cut into 2-inch pieces,
   crisp-cooked, and drained
3 cups shredded cheddar cheese
   (12 ounces)

Grease two 12-inch pizza pans. Prepare purchased crusts according to package directions. (If using Homemade Pizza Crusts, on lightly floured surface, roll each half of the dough into a 13-inch circle; transfer to pans. Build up edges. Prick with fork. Do not let rise. Bake in a 425° oven for 10 to 12 minutes or until golden.) Cook beef and onion until meat is brown. Drain off fat. Spread Hunt's Ready Tomato Sauces Chunky Italian over crusts. Top with beef mixture. Top with remaining ingredients. Bake purchased crusts according to package directions or bake homemade crusts in a 425° oven about 12 minutes more or until cheese melts.

Nutrition facts per serving: 540 cal., 32 g pro., 39 g carbo.,
27 g fat, 91 mg chol., 2 g dietary fiber, 1,043 mg sodium.

HOMEMADE PIZZA CRUSTS

Measure 3¼ cups *all-purpose flour*. Mix 1¼ *cups* of the flour, 1 package *active dry yeast*, and ¼ teaspoon *salt*. Add 1 cup *warm water* (120° to 130°) and 2 tablespoons *Wesson® Oil*. Beat with electric mixer on low speed for 30 seconds, scraping the bowl constantly. Beat on high speed for 3 minutes. Use a spoon to stir in as much of the remaining flour as you can. Turn onto a lightly floured surface. Knead in enough of remaining flour to make a moderately stiff dough that is smooth and elastic (6 to 8 minutes total). Divide in half. Cover; let rest 10 minutes. Continue as directed in pizza recipes. Makes 2 crusts.

Vegetable Lasagna

Makes 8 Servings
Prep Time: 45 Minutes • Cook Time: 30 Minutes

9 lasagna noodles
2 tablespoons margarine or butter
1 cup chopped fresh mushrooms
1 large onion, chopped
1 large green pepper, chopped
2 medium carrots, chopped
4 cloves garlic, minced
4 cups chopped broccoli
   (flowerets and stems)
½ cup water
1 15-ounce container ricotta cheese
1 cup shredded mozzarella cheese
   (4 ounces)

½ cup grated Parmesan
   or Romano cheese
2 eggs
¼ cup snipped parsley
½ teaspoon dried thyme, crushed
½ teaspoon dried marjoram, crushed
¼ teaspoon black pepper
1 27-ounce can Hunt's® Classic Italian
   Spaghetti Sauce with Garlic and Herb
¼ cup grated Parmesan
   or Romano cheese

Cook lasagna noodles according to package directions. Drain; set aside. Melt margarine in a large skillet. Cook and stir mushrooms, onion, green pepper, carrots, and garlic in melted margarine until vegetables are tender. Add broccoli and water. Bring to boiling; reduce heat. Simmer, covered, about 5 minutes or until broccoli is crisp-tender; remove from heat and set aside. Mix ricotta, mozzarella, the ½ cup Parmesan, eggs, parsley, thyme, marjoram, and black pepper; set aside.

Evenly spread ½ *cup* of the Hunt's Classic Italian Spaghetti Sauce with Garlic and Herb in a 3-quart rectangular baking dish. Arrange 3 lasagna noodles over sauce. Layer with *half* of the cheese mixture, *half* of the vegetable mixture, *1 cup* of the spaghetti sauce, and 3 more noodles. Repeat with layers of cheese and vegetable mixtures, *1 cup* spaghetti sauce, and 3 more noodles. Spoon remaining spaghetti sauce over the top. Sprinkle with the ¼ cup Parmesan cheese.

Bake, covered, in a 375° oven for 20 minutes. Uncover and bake about 10 minutes more or until heated through.

Nutrition facts per serving: 387 cal., 23 g pro., 40 g carbo.,
16 g fat, 85 mg chol., 5 g dietary fiber, 831 mg sodium.

Baked Cavatelli

MAKES 6 SERVINGS
PREP TIME: 30 MINUTES • COOK TIME: 30 MINUTES

2½ cups packaged dried wagon-wheel macaroni

¾ pound Italian sausage links, cut into ½-inch slices

¾ cup chopped green onions

2 cloves garlic, minced

1 27-ounce can Hunt's® Original Spaghetti Sauce with Mushrooms*

1 cup shredded mozzarella cheese (4 ounces)

1 teaspoon dried Italian seasoning, crushed

¼ teaspoon pepper

Cook the macaroni according to package directions. Drain; set aside.

Meanwhile, cook sausage in a large skillet until no pink remains; remove sausage from skillet. Drain off fat, reserving 1 *tablespoon* in skillet. Cook green onions and garlic in skillet until onions are tender. Drain off fat.

Combine cooked pasta, cooked sausage, onion mixture, Hunt's Original Spaghetti Sauce with Mushrooms, *half* of the mozzarella cheese, the Italian seasoning, and pepper in a 2-quart casserole.

Bake, covered, in a 375° oven for 25 minutes. Uncover; sprinkle with remaining mozzarella cheese. Bake for 5 to 10 minutes more or until heated through.

*Note: Store the leftover spaghetti sauce in a tightly covered plastic container in the refrigerator for up to 1 week.

Nutrition facts per serving: 379 cal., 20 g pro., 45 g carbo., 14 g fat, 39 mg chol., 2 g dietary fiber, 791 mg sodium.

SENSATIONAL SNACKING

Keep that leftover Hunt's® Spaghetti Sauce in mind the next time you're hungry for a snack. The sauce works wonders when you spread it on toasted English muffins or bagel halves, sprinkle it with shredded mozzarella or Monterey Jack cheese, then heat it under the broiler until the cheese melts.

SHORTCUT LASAGNA

MAKES 8 SERVINGS
PREP TIME: 35 MINUTES • COOK TIME: 40 MINUTES

½ pound ground beef
½ pound bulk Italian sausage
1 15-ounce can Hunt's® Tomato Sauce
1 14½-ounce can Hunt's Stewed Tomatoes
1 6-ounce can Hunt's Tomato Paste
1½ teaspoons dried Italian seasoning, crushed

½ teaspoon pepper
1 egg
1 pint (2 cups) ricotta cheese or cream-style cottage cheese
9 no-boil lasagna noodles
1 8-ounce package sliced mozzarella cheese
¼ cup grated Parmesan cheese

Cook ground beef and Italian sausage in a large skillet until brown. Drain off fat. Stir in Hunt's Tomato Sauce, *undrained* Hunt's Stewed Tomatoes, Hunt's Tomato Paste, Italian seasoning, and pepper; bring to boiling.

Meanwhile, use a fork to beat egg slightly in a mixing bowl. Stir in ricotta or cottage cheese.

To assemble, spread about *1 cup* of the hot meat mixture in the bottom of a 3-quart rectangular baking dish. Place 3 no-boil lasagna noodles on top of meat mixture, making sure the noodles do not touch the edges of the dish. Spread noodles with another *1 cup* of the meat mixture. Then top with *one-third* of the ricotta mixture and *one-third* of the mozzarella cheese. Repeat twice more with layers of no-boil noodles, meat mixture, ricotta mixture, and mozzarella cheese. Sprinkle with Parmesan cheese. Cover with foil.

Bake in a 350° oven for 30 minutes. Uncover and bake for 10 to 15 minutes more or until mozzarella cheese is melted and noodles are tender. Let stand about 5 minutes before serving.

*Nutrition facts per serving: 440 cal., 37 g pro., 32 g carbo.,
20 g fat, 98 mg chol., 2 g dietary fiber, 986 mg sodium.*

MEATBALL HERO SANDWICHES

MAKES 4 SERVINGS
TOTAL TIME: 45 MINUTES

½ **pound ground beef**	1 **15-ounce can Hunt's® Ready Tomato**
¼ **pound bulk hot Italian sausage**	**Sauces Original Italian**
¼ **cup fine dry seasoned bread crumbs**	1 **teaspoon sugar**
1 **beaten egg**	2 **tablespoons grated Parmesan cheese**
	4 **6-inch hoagie buns, split and toasted**

Combine ground beef, Italian sausage, bread crumbs, and egg in a small mixing bowl. Shape mixture into twelve 1½-inch balls.* Place meatballs on a foil-lined baking sheet. Bake in a 375° oven for 25 minutes; drain meatballs on paper towels.

Combine Hunt's Ready Tomato Sauces Original Italian and sugar in a large saucepan. Stir in meatballs. Bring to boiling; reduce heat. Simmer, covered, for 10 minutes. Stir in cheese. Spoon 3 meatballs and some of the sauce into each bun.

***Note:** To shape even-size meatballs, mold the meat mixture into a log about 1½ inches in diameter. Cut log into 12 even slices. With your hands, shape each slice into a smooth ball.

Nutrition facts per serving: 493 cal., 29 g pro., 52 g carbo., 19 g fat, 115 mg chol., 4 g dietary fiber, 1,281 mg sodium.

DOUBLE-DUTY MEATBALLS

Next time you make the sandwiches *above*, double the meatball recipe and freeze half after baking, so you can have another homemade meal on your table in minutes. To serve, heat two cans of your favorite Hunt's® Ready Tomato Sauces in a large saucepan. Add the frozen meatballs and simmer over medium-low heat about 20 minutes or until the meatballs are heated through, stirring often. Spoon the meatballs and sauce over mounds of hot cooked spaghetti or other pasta.

SAVORY SHEPHERD'S PIE

MAKES 4 SERVINGS
PREP TIME: 35 MINUTES • COOK TIME: 25 MINUTES

3 small potatoes (½ pound)*
2 tablespoons margarine or butter
2 cloves garlic, minced
½ teaspoon dried basil, crushed
¼ teaspoon salt
2 to 4 tablespoons milk
1 tablespoon Wesson® Oil
1 medium onion, chopped
1 medium carrot, sliced
1 15-ounce can kidney beans, rinsed
    and drained

1 14½-ounce can Hunt's® Choice-Cut™
    Diced Tomatoes
1 10-ounce package frozen
    whole kernel corn
1 8-ounce can Hunt's Tomato Sauce
1 teaspoon Worcestershire sauce
½ teaspoon sugar
1 cup shredded cheddar cheese
    (4 ounces)

Peel and quarter potatoes. Cook, covered, in a small amount of boiling lightly salted water for 20 to 25 minutes or until tender. Drain. Mash with potato masher or beat with an electric mixer on low speed. Melt margarine in a small saucepan. Cook garlic and basil in melted margarine for 15 seconds. Add to mashed potatoes along with salt. Gradually beat in enough of the milk to make light and fluffy. Set aside.

For filling, heat Wesson Oil in a large skillet. Cook and stir onion and carrot in hot oil until onion is tender. Stir in kidney beans, *undrained* Hunt's Choice-Cut Diced Tomatoes, frozen corn, Hunt's Tomato Sauce, Worcestershire sauce, and sugar; bring to boiling. Transfer to an 8x8x2-inch baking pan. Drop mashed potatoes in 4 mounds onto vegetable mixture. Sprinkle with cheddar cheese. Bake, uncovered, in a 375° oven for 25 to 30 minutes or until heated through and cheese begins to brown.

*Note: You can substitute packaged instant mashed potatoes for the 3 small potatoes. Prepare 4 servings of potatoes according to package directions and stir in the garlic mixture. Make filling, assemble, and bake as directed *above*.

Nutrition facts per serving: 462 cal., 18 g pro., 59 g carbo., 19 g fat, 30 mg chol., 12 g dietary fiber, 1,277 mg sodium.

ROASTED FISH WITH TOMATOES AND CHEESE

MAKES 4 SERVINGS
PREP TIME: 25 MINUTES • COOK TIME: 8 MINUTES

1 **pound fresh or frozen red snapper fillets, cut about 1 inch thick**	1 **teaspoon dried oregano, crushed** **Wesson® No Stick Cooking Spray**
1 **14½-ounce can Hunt's® Choice-Cut™ Diced Tomatoes**	¼ **teaspoon pepper**
8 **green onions, sliced (½ cup)**	¼ **teaspoon ground coriander**
¼ **cup thinly sliced celery**	¼ **cup crumbled feta cheese (1 ounce)**
2 **tablespoons lemon juice**	2 **tablespoons sliced ripe olives**

Thaw fish, if frozen. Rinse fish. Cut fish into 4 portions.

For sauce, combine *undrained* Hunt's Choice-Cut Diced Tomatoes, green onions, celery, lemon juice, and oregano in a large skillet. Bring to boiling; reduce heat. Simmer, uncovered, about 15 minutes or until most of the liquid has evaporated.

Meanwhile, spray a 2-quart rectangular baking dish with Wesson No Stick Cooking Spray. Place fish fillets in the baking dish, tucking under any thin edges. Sprinkle with pepper and coriander.

Bake, uncovered, in a 450° oven for 8 to 10 minutes or until fish flakes easily when tested with a fork.

Transfer fish to individual serving plates. Spoon sauce over fish. Sprinkle feta cheese and olives over fish.

Nutrition facts per serving: 159 cal., 25 g pro., 6 g carbo., 4 g fat, 46 mg chol., 1 g dietary fiber, 406 mg sodium.

SHORTCUT SOUPS AND STEWS

Thanks to the convenience of Hunt's® tomato products, you can offer your family a splendid array of flavorful soups and stews—from smooth to chunky, subtly flavored to bold—all in a matter of minutes. When you sample any one of these recipes, you'll see why home-cooked comfort foods are welcome any day.

Snapper and Pasta Stew (see recipe, page 50)

SNAPPER AND PASTA STEW

MAKES 4 SERVINGS
TOTAL TIME: 40 MINUTES

1 **pound fresh or frozen skinless red snapper or rockfish fillets**	2 **tablespoons snipped fresh basil or 1 teaspoon dried basil, crushed**
2 **tablespoons Wesson® Oil**	1 **teaspoon snipped fresh rosemary or ¼ teaspoon dried rosemary, crushed**
6 **medium leeks, sliced**	¼ **teaspoon salt**
1 **medium green pepper, cut into strips**	¼ **teaspoon black pepper**
1 **medium yellow or red sweet pepper, cut into strips**	1 **cup packaged dried medium shell macaroni**
2 **cloves garlic, minced**	¼ **cup sliced pitted ripe olives**
1 **14½-ounce can Hunt's® Whole Tomatoes, cut up**	**Fresh rosemary (optional)**
1¼ **cups water**	**Sliced pitted ripe olives (optional)**

Thaw fish fillets, if frozen. Rinse fish.

Heat Wesson Oil in a large saucepan. Cook and stir leeks, green pepper, yellow or red pepper, and garlic in hot oil until vegetables are crisp-tender. Stir in *undrained* Hunt's Whole Tomatoes (cut up), water, basil, rosemary, salt, and black pepper. Bring mixture to boiling. Add *uncooked* macaroni. Reduce heat; simmer, covered, about 15 minutes or until macaroni is tender.

Meanwhile, cut fish into 1-inch cubes. Add fish and the ¼ cup olives to tomato mixture. Return to boiling; reduce heat. Simmer, covered, for 4 to 6 minutes or until fish flakes easily when tested with a fork. Garnish with fresh rosemary and additional sliced olives, if desired.

Nutrition facts per serving: 342 cal., 28 g pro., 36 g carbo., 10 g fat, 40 mg chol., 4 g dietary fiber, 536 mg sodium.

Note: Pictured on pages 48–49.

IOPPINO

MAKES 4 SERVINGS
TOTAL TIME: 35 MINUTES

½	**pound fresh or frozen fish fillets**
I	**medium green or red sweet pepper, chopped**
I	**medium onion, chopped**
¼	**cup water**
I	**clove garlic, minced**
I	**14½-ounce can Hunt's® Choice-Cut™ Diced Tomatoes**
I	**8-ounce can Hunt's Tomato Sauce**

½	**cup dry red or white wine**
2	**tablespoons snipped parsley**
¼	**teaspoon salt**
¼	**teaspoon dried oregano, crushed**
¼	**teaspoon dried basil, crushed**
⅛	**teaspoon black pepper**
I	**6½-ounce can minced clams**
¾	**cup frozen, peeled, cooked shrimp (3 ounces)**

Thaw fish, if frozen. Rinse fish. Cut fish into 1-inch pieces; set aside. Stir together green or red sweet pepper, onion, water, and garlic in a large saucepan. Bring to boiling; reduce heat. Simmer, covered, for 3 to 4 minutes or until the vegetables are tender.

Stir in *undrained* Hunt's Choice-Cut Diced Tomatoes, Hunt's Tomato Sauce, red or white wine, parsley, salt, oregano, basil, and black pepper. Bring to boiling; reduce heat. Simmer, covered, for 10 minutes.

Add fish, *undrained* clams, and frozen shrimp. Bring just to boiling; reduce heat. Simmer, covered, for 4 to 5 minutes or until fish flakes easily when tested with a fork and shrimp are heated through.

Nutrition facts per serving: 171 cal., 23 g pro., 11 g carbo.,
1 g fat, 82 mg chol., 3 g dietary fiber, 856 mg sodium.

Two-Way Minestrone

MAKES 4 SERVINGS
TOTAL TIME: 25 MINUTES

¾ pound fresh or frozen fish fillets
   (cod, pike, or orange roughy),
   turkey breast tenderloin steaks,
   or skinless, boneless chicken
   breast halves

2 14½-ounce cans chicken broth

1 15-ounce can garbanzo or kidney
   beans, rinsed and drained

1 cup loose-pack frozen
   mixed vegetables

1 medium onion, chopped

½ cup packaged dried cavatelli
   or small pasta (shells, wheels,
   or macaroni)

1 teaspoon dried basil or thyme,
   crushed

¼ teaspoon pepper

1 14½-ounce can Hunt's® Stewed
   Tomatoes

¼ teaspoon dried Italian seasoning,
   crushed

Thaw fish fillets, if frozen. Remove skin. Rinse fish or poultry. Cut fish or poultry into 1-inch pieces; set aside.

Stir together broth, garbanzo or kidney beans, frozen mixed vegetables, onion, *uncooked* pasta, basil or thyme, and pepper in a large saucepan. Bring to boiling; reduce heat. Simmer, covered, for 10 minutes.

Stir in *undrained* Hunt's Stewed Tomatoes and Italian seasoning. Add fish or poultry pieces. Return to boiling; reduce heat. Simmer, covered, until fish flakes easily when tested with a fork or poultry is tender and no longer pink, stirring once. (For fish, allow 2 to 3 minutes; for poultry, allow 4 to 5 minutes.)

Nutrition facts per serving: 351 cal., 28 g pro., 46 g carbo., 6 g fat, 37 mg chol., 26 g dietary fiber, 1,516 mg sodium.

CURRIED CHICKEN SOUP

MAKES 3 OR 4 SERVINGS
TOTAL TIME: 20 MINUTES

2 tablespoons Wesson® Oil
1 cup loose-pack frozen crinkle-cut carrots
¼ cup sliced green onions
1 teaspoon curry powder
3 cups chicken broth

1 14½-ounce can Hunt's® Whole Tomatoes, cut up
1 teaspoon dried basil, crushed
⅛ teaspoon ground red pepper
¾ cup instant mashed potato flakes
2 5-ounce cans chunk-style chicken, flaked

Heat Wesson Oil in a large saucepan. Cook frozen carrots, green onions, and curry powder in hot oil, stirring often, for 3 to 4 minutes or until carrots are crisp-tender. Stir in broth, *undrained* Hunt's Whole Tomatoes (cut up), basil, and ground red pepper. Bring to boiling; reduce heat. Stir in potato flakes and *undrained* chicken; heat about 2 minutes more or until mixture is slightly thickened.

Nutrition facts per serving: 358 cal., 26 g pro., 22 g carbo., 19 g fat, 59 mg chol., 4 g dietary fiber, 1,854 mg sodium.

SOUPER TOPPERS

A crunchy accompaniment turns a simple bowl of soup into a memorable meal.

For a flavorful cracker mix to sprinkle on soups, combine 1 cup *bite-size fish-shaped cheese-flavored crackers,* 1 cup *oyster crackers,* 1 cup *bite-size shredded wheat biscuits,* and 1 cup *miniature rich round crackers.* Combine 2 tablespoons Wesson® *Oil,* ½ teaspoon *Worcestershire sauce,* ⅛ teaspoon *garlic powder,* and dash bottled *hot pepper sauce;* toss with crackers. Toss with 2 tablespoons grated *Parmesan cheese.* Spread on a shallow baking sheet. Bake in a 300° oven for 10 to 15 minutes or until golden, stirring once. Cool. Store in an airtight container for up to 2 weeks.

Or, float croutons, popcorn, or toasted French bread rounds on soups.

Easy Hamburger-Vegetable Soup

MAKES 4 SERVINGS
TOTAL TIME: 35 MINUTES

-   1   pound ground beef or ground pork
-   ½   cup chopped onion
-   ½   cup chopped green pepper
-   3   cups beef broth*
-   1   14½-ounce can Hunt's® Whole Tomatoes, cut up
-   1   cup frozen whole kernel corn
-   ½   of a 9-ounce package frozen lima beans
-   ½   cup chopped, peeled potato or loose-pack frozen hash brown potatoes
-   1   medium carrot, cut into julienne strips
-   1   tablespoon snipped fresh basil or 1 teaspoon dried basil, crushed
-   1   teaspoon Worcestershire sauce
-   ⅛   teaspoon black pepper
-   1   bay leaf

Cook ground beef or pork, onion, and green pepper in a large saucepan or Dutch oven until meat is brown and onion is tender. Drain off fat.

Stir in beef broth, *undrained* Hunt's Whole Tomatoes (cut up), frozen corn, frozen lima beans, potato, carrot, basil, Worcestershire sauce, black pepper, and bay leaf. Bring to boiling; reduce heat. Simmer, covered, for 15 to 20 minutes or until vegetables are tender. Discard bay leaf.

Note: Use homemade or canned beef broth, or add 1 tablespoon instant beef bouillon granules to 3 cups boiling water and stir until dissolved.

Nutrition facts per serving: 400 cal., 32 g pro., 30 g carbo., 17 g fat, 84 mg chol., 7 g dietary fiber, 1,010 mg sodium.

TURKEY-RICE SOUP

MAKES 6 SERVINGS
TOTAL TIME: 35 MINUTES

4 cups chicken broth	1 cup quick-cooking rice
¼ teaspoon dried rosemary, crushed	2 cups chopped cooked turkey or chicken
1 10-ounce package frozen mixed vegetables (2 cups)	1 14½-ounce can Hunt's® Whole Tomatoes, cut up

Combine broth, rosemary, 1 cup *water*, and ¼ teaspoon *pepper* in a large saucepan. Bring to boiling. Stir in frozen mixed vegetables and *uncooked* rice. Return to boiling; reduce heat. Simmer, covered, for 15 minutes. Stir in turkey and *undrained* Hunt's Whole Tomatoes (cut up); heat through.

Nutrition facts per serving: 207 cal., 19 g pro., 25 g carbo.,
4 g fat, 35 mg chol., 3 g dietary fiber, 880 mg sodium.

CLAM CHOWDER

MAKES 4 SERVINGS
TOTAL TIME: 40 MINUTES

2 6½-ounce cans minced clams Wesson® No Stick Cooking Spray	1 cup chopped onion
2 slices turkey bacon, chopped	½ teaspoon dried basil or marjoram, crushed
2 cups finely chopped, peeled potatoes (2 medium)	2 14½-ounce cans Hunt's® Whole Tomatoes, cut up
1 cup chopped celery	

Drain clams, reserving juice. If necessary, add water to juice to equal *1½ cups*. Set aside. Spray a *cold* large saucepan with Wesson No Stick Cooking Spray. Preheat over medium heat. Cook bacon in hot pan until brown; remove and set aside. Drain off fat. Stir clam juice, vegetables, basil, and ¼ teaspoon *pepper* into saucepan. Bring to boiling; reduce heat. Simmer, covered, for 10 to 15 minutes or until the vegetables are tender. Stir in *undrained* Hunt's Whole Tomatoes (cut up); heat through. Use a fork to slightly mash vegetables. Stir in clams; heat through. Top with bacon.

Nutrition facts per serving: 199 cal., 17 g pro., 27 g carbo.,
2 g fat, 38 mg chol., 3 g dietary fiber, 833 mg sodium.

Sausage-Vegetable Soup

Makes 4 Servings
Total Time: 50 Minutes

- ¾ pound bulk Italian sausage
- ½ cup chopped onion
- 3 cups beef broth*
- 1 14½-ounce can Hunt's® Choice-Cut™ Diced Tomatoes
- 1 cup thinly sliced carrot
- 1 tablespoon snipped fresh basil or 1 teaspoon dried basil, crushed
- 1 tablespoon snipped parsley
- 2 cloves garlic, minced
- ⅛ teaspoon pepper
- 1 cup sliced zucchini or yellow summer squash
- 1 cup packaged dried rotini or small shell macaroni
- ¼ cup grated Parmesan cheese

Cook Italian sausage and onion in a large saucepan or Dutch oven until sausage no longer is pink and onion is tender. Pour sausage mixture into a colander to drain off fat; rinse sausage mixture and drain again.

Return sausage mixture to saucepan or Dutch oven. Stir in beef broth, *undrained* Hunt's Choice-Cut Diced Tomatoes, carrot, basil, parsley, garlic, and pepper. Bring to boiling; reduce heat. Simmer, covered, for 10 minutes. Stir in zucchini and *uncooked* pasta. Return to boiling; reduce heat. Simmer, covered, for 10 to 15 minutes more or until pasta and vegetables are tender. Sprinkle with Parmesan cheese.

Note: Use homemade or canned beef broth, or add 1 tablespoon instant beef bouillon granules to 3 cups boiling water and stir until dissolved.

Nutrition facts per serving: 381 cal., 21 g pro., 34 g carbo., 18 g fat, 49 mg chol., 3 g dietary fiber, 1,527 mg sodium.

CHICKEN GUMBO

MAKES 6 SERVINGS
TOTAL TIME: 50 MINUTES

2 tablespoons Wesson® Oil
1 cup chopped onion
½ cup sliced celery
½ cup chopped green pepper
2 cloves garlic, minced
3 cups water
1 15-ounce can Hunt's® Tomato Sauce
1 14½-ounce can chicken broth
1 14½-ounce can Hunt's Choice-Cut™ Diced Tomatoes

1½ cups chopped, cooked chicken
1 cup fresh or frozen sliced okra
⅓ cup long-grain rice
1 teaspoon bottled hot pepper sauce
½ teaspoon dried thyme, crushed
½ teaspoon dried basil, crushed
½ teaspoon filé powder
1 bay leaf

Heat Wesson Oil in large saucepan or Dutch oven. Cook and stir onion, celery, green pepper, and garlic in hot oil until vegetables are tender. Stir in water, Hunt's Tomato Sauce, broth, *undrained* Hunt's Choice-Cut Diced Tomatoes, chicken, okra, *uncooked* rice, hot pepper sauce, thyme, basil, filé powder, and bay leaf. Bring to boiling; reduce heat. Simmer, uncovered, for 20 minutes. Discard bay leaf.

Nutrition facts per serving: 200 cal., 15 g pro., 20 g carbo., 7 g fat, 30 mg chol., 3 g dietary fiber, 913 mg sodium.

TANTALIZING TURKEY SOUP

Wondering what to do with leftovers from that holiday turkey? Create a full-flavored soup by heating together 2 cups diced cooked *turkey*, 2 cups cooked *vegetables*, two 14½-ounce cans *Hunt's® Choice-Cut™ Diced Tomatoes*, 2 cups *water*, 1 teaspoon dried *Italian seasoning*, crushed, and ¼ teaspoon *onion powder*. If desired, stir in 1 cup *cooked pasta* or *barley* and heat through.

Pasta-Bean Soup with Fresh Herbs

MAKES 4 SERVINGS
TOTAL TIME: 30 MINUTES

- 1 tablespoon margarine or butter
- 2 cups sliced fresh mushrooms
- 1 medium onion, chopped
- 2 cloves garlic, minced
- 2 14½-ounce cans vegetable, chicken, or beef broth
- ½ cup packaged dried small shell macaroni
- 1 15-ounce can garbanzo beans, rinsed and drained
- 1 14½-ounce can Hunt's® Whole Tomatoes, cut up
- ¼ cup snipped fresh basil
- 1 tablespoon snipped fresh thyme
- Fresh basil sprigs (optional)

Melt margarine in large saucepan or Dutch oven. Cook and stir mushrooms, onion, and garlic in melted margarine until vegetables are tender but not brown. Add broth. Bring to boiling; stir in *uncooked* macaroni. Return to boiling; cook for 10 to 12 minutes or until macaroni is just tender. Stir in garbanzo beans and *undrained* Hunt's Whole Tomatoes (cut up); heat through.

Just before serving, stir in the ¼ cup fresh basil and the thyme. Garnish with fresh basil sprigs, if desired.

Nutrition facts per serving: 234 cal., 9 g pro., 38 g carbo., 6 g fat, 0 mg chol., 6 g dietary fiber, 1,361 mg sodium.

NO SALT ADDED

If you're trying to trim sodium in your diet, choose Hunt's® No Salt Added products. When substituting the no-salt-added versions of whole tomatoes, tomato sauce, tomato paste, stewed tomatoes, and tomato juice, use the same amount as the recipe specifies. Then, you may want to slightly increase the other seasonings.

READY-IN-MINUTES MICROWAVE MEALS

What could be faster than a microwave meal made with convenient Hunt's® tomato products. From homestyle soups and sauces to Tex-Mex fare, you'll create entrées that go from the microwave to "More, please!" in minutes.

Turkey and Shrimp Jambalaya (see recipe, page 64)

Turkey and Shrimp Jambalaya

Makes 4 Servings
Total Time: 35 Minutes

1	14½-ounce can Hunt's® Whole Tomatoes, cut up
1	cup finely chopped onion
½	cup chicken broth
2	tablespoons Hunt's Tomato Paste
3	cloves garlic, minced
1	bay leaf
1	teaspoon dried Italian seasoning, crushed
½	teaspoon salt
½	teaspoon chili powder

¼	teaspoon black pepper
	Few dashes bottled hot pepper sauce
1½	cups chopped green pepper
1	cup quick-cooking rice
¾	pound medium shrimp in shells, peeled, deveined, and halved lengthwise
¼	pound smoked turkey sausage, cut into ¼-inch slices and halved
	Lemon wedges (optional)

Combine *undrained* Hunt's Whole Tomatoes (cut up), onion, broth, Hunt's Tomato Paste, garlic, bay leaf, Italian seasoning, salt, chili powder, black pepper, and hot pepper sauce in a 3-quart microwave-safe casserole. Cover; micro-cook on 100% power (high) for 5 minutes. Stir in green pepper. Cover; cook on high for 2 minutes. Stir in *uncooked* rice, shrimp, and sausage. Cover; cook on high for 3 to 5 minutes more or until shrimp just turn pink, stirring once. Let stand, covered, for 1 to 2 minutes or until rice is tender. Remove bay leaf. Serve in bowls with lemon wedges, if desired.

Nutrition facts per serving: 233 cal., 18 g pro., 32 g carbo., 5 g fat, 81 mg chol., 3 g dietary fiber, 982 mg sodium.

Note: Pictured on pages 62–63.

Fish-Vegetable Medley

Makes 4 Servings
Total Time: 25 Minutes

I pound fresh or frozen skinless sole or flounder fillets, cut ½ inch thick	I clove garlic, minced
I small yellow summer squash	I 14½-ounce can Hunt's® Whole Tomatoes, cut up
I small zucchini	I tablespoon cornstarch
I cup sliced fresh mushrooms	¼ teaspoon dried basil, crushed
½ of a small onion, sliced and separated into rings	¼ teaspoon dried oregano, crushed
	Dash bottled hot pepper sauce

Thaw fish, if frozen. Rinse fish. For sauce, cut yellow squash and zucchini in half lengthwise, then crosswise into ¼-inch-thick slices. Combine squash, zucchini, mushrooms, onion, garlic, and 2 tablespoons *water* in a 2-quart microwave-safe casserole. Cover; micro-cook on 100% power (high) for 4½ to 5 minutes or until vegetables are nearly tender, stirring once. Drain. Combine *undrained* Hunt's Whole Tomatoes (cut up), cornstarch, basil, oregano, and hot pepper sauce. Stir into vegetables. Cook, uncovered, on high for 4 to 6 minutes or until bubbly, stirring every 2 minutes. Cook 1 minute more. Arrange fish in an 8x8x2-inch microwave-safe baking dish; turn under thin portions. Cover with vented clear plastic wrap. Cook on high for 4 to 7 minutes or until fish flakes easily when tested with a fork; give dish a half-turn once. Serve sauce over fish.

Nutrition facts per serving: 142 cal., 22 g pro., 9 g carbo.,
2 g fat, 58 mg chol., 2 g dietary fiber, 370 mg sodium.

Microwave Oven Wattage

All of the recipes in this chapter were tested in a variety of high-wattage microwave ovens. The cooking times for these recipes are approximate because microwave ovens vary by manufacturer. For best results, check the food at the end of the minimum cooking time given in the recipe. Then continue cooking as needed.

Super Chunky Pasta Sauce

Makes 4 Servings
Total Time: 20 Minutes

1 **pound ground beef**	1 **14½-ounce can Hunt's Choice-Cut™**
½ **cup chopped onion**	**Diced Tomatoes**
1½ **cups sliced fresh mushrooms**	2 **tablespoons snipped parsley**
1 **cup chopped green pepper**	½ **pound packaged dried mostaccioli or**
1 **15-ounce can Hunt's® Ready Tomato**	**fettuccine, cooked and drained**
Sauces Chunky Garlic and Herb	**Freshly grated Parmesan cheese**

Crumble meat into a 2-quart microwave-safe casserole; stir in onion. Cover; micro-cook on 100% power (high) for 5 to 7 minutes or until meat no longer is pink, stirring once. Drain meat; set aside. Wipe out casserole with paper towels. Combine mushrooms, green pepper, Hunt's Ready Tomato Sauces Chunky Garlic and Herb, and Hunt's Choice-Cut Diced Tomatoes in the same casserole. Cover; cook on high for 7 to 9 minutes or until vegetables are crisp-tender. Stir in meat mixture and parsley. Cover; cook on high for 1 to 2 minutes or until heated through. Serve over hot cooked pasta. Sprinkle with Parmesan cheese.

Nutrition facts per serving: 585 cal., 38 g pro., 62 g carbo.,
19 g fat, 101 mg chol., 4 g dietary fiber, 741 mg sodium.

Saucy Baked Potatoes

Baked potatoes take on a whole new dimension when you top them with Hunt's® Ready Tomato Sauces. The sauces are nearly fat free, full of flavor, and more healthful than traditional potato toppers such as margarine, butter, or sour cream. Choose any of the rich Ready Tomato Sauces blends to turn a baked potato into a quick and easy, one-dish meal. (See the recipe on *page 75* for microwave directions for baked potatoes.)

Taco Casserole

MAKES 6 SERVINGS
TOTAL TIME: 25 MINUTES

1	pound ground beef
½	cup chopped onion
1	15-ounce can pinto beans, rinsed and drained
1	8-ounce can Hunt's® Tomato Sauce
¼	cup Hunt's Ready Tomato Sauces Chunky Salsa*
1	teaspoon chili powder
1½	cups shredded Monterey Jack or mozzarella cheese (6 ounces)
2	cups broken tortilla chips
1	cup shredded lettuce
¼	cup sliced green onions
¼	cup sliced pitted ripe olives
1	6-ounce container frozen avocado dip, thawed

Crumble meat into a 1½-quart microwave-safe casserole; stir in chopped onion. Cover; micro-cook on 100% power (high) for 4½ to 5½ minutes or until meat no longer is pink, stirring once. Drain off fat. Stir in pinto beans, Hunt's Tomato Sauce, Hunt's Ready Tomato Sauces Chunky Salsa, and chili powder. Cover; cook on high about 6 minutes or until bubbly.

Top with shredded cheese. Cook, uncovered, on high about 1 minute more or until cheese is melted. Top with broken tortilla chips and lettuce. Garnish with green onions, olives, and thawed avocado dip.

*Note: Store the leftover chunky salsa sauce in a tightly covered plastic container in the refrigerator for up to 1 week. See the tips on pages 14, 21, 27, and 66 for ideas on how to use the leftover sauce.

Nutrition facts per serving: 465 cal., 30 g pro., 24 g carbo., 29 g fat, 82 mg chol., 7 g dietary fiber, 786 mg sodium.

Shortcut Stuffed Manicotti

Makes 4 Servings
Total Time: 45 Minutes

½ pound ground beef	1¼ cups water
½ of a 16-ounce can (1 cup) refried beans	1 8-ounce can Hunt's® Tomato Sauce
1 teaspoon dried oregano, crushed	½ cup shredded Monterey Jack or cheddar cheese (2 ounces)
½ teaspoon ground cumin	½ cup dairy sour cream
8 packaged dried manicotti shells	¼ cup finely chopped green onions

Combine meat, refried beans, oregano, and cumin in a medium mixing bowl; mix well. Spoon meat mixture into *uncooked* manicotti shells. Arrange filled shells in a 2-quart rectangular microwave-safe baking dish. Combine water and Hunt's Tomato Sauce; pour over manicotti.

Cover with vented clear plastic wrap. Micro-cook on 100% power (high) for 10 minutes, giving the dish a half-turn once. Turn manicotti over. Cover; cook on 50% power (medium) for 17 to 19 minutes or until manicotti is tender, giving the dish a half-turn once.

Top with shredded cheese. Cook, uncovered, on high about 1 minute or until cheese melts. Combine sour cream and green onions. Spoon over manicotti.

Nutrition facts per serving: 411 cal., 25 g pro., 34 g carbo., 19 g fat, 68 mg chol., 6 g dietary fiber, 720 mg sodium.

Easy Beef Casserole

MAKES 4 SERVINGS
TOTAL TIME: 15 MINUTES

¾ pound ground beef
2 medium carrots, thinly sliced
1 cup frozen whole kernel corn
1 medium onion, chopped

1 15-ounce can Hunt's® Ready Tomato
   Sauces Chunky Chili
½ cup shredded cheddar cheese
   (2 ounces)

Crumble meat into a 1½-quart microwave-safe casserole; stir in carrots, frozen corn, and onion. Cover; micro-cook on 100% power (high) for 4 to 6 minutes or until meat no longer is pink, stirring twice. Drain off fat. Stir in Hunt's Ready Tomato Sauces Chunky Chili. Cover; cook on high for 4 to 5 minutes or until bubbly, stirring twice. Top with cheese.

Nutrition facts per serving: 333 cal., 26 g pro., 21 g carbo.,
17 g fat, 78 mg chol., 4 g dietary fiber, 688 mg sodium.

Chili

MAKES 4 SERVINGS
TOTAL TIME: 25 MINUTES

¾ pound ground beef
1 cup chopped onion
½ cup chopped green pepper
2 cloves garlic, minced
1 16-ounce can dark red kidney beans,
   drained

1 14½-ounce can Hunt's® Whole
   Tomatoes, cut up
1 8-ounce can Hunt's Tomato Sauce
2 to 3 teaspoons chili powder
½ teaspoon dried basil, crushed
¼ teaspoon salt
¼ teaspoon black pepper

Mix first 4 ingredients in a 2-quart microwave-safe casserole. Cover; micro-cook on 100% power (high) for 6 to 9 minutes or until meat no longer is pink, stirring once. Drain off fat. Stir in remaining ingredients. Cover; cook on high for 9 to 11 minutes or until heated through, stirring twice.

Nutrition facts per serving: 331 cal., 27 g pro., 28 g carbo.,
13 g fat, 63 mg chol., 9 g dietary fiber, 1,164 mg sodium.

EEF BURRITOS

MAKES 4 SERVINGS
TOTAL TIME: 35 MINUTES

¾	pound ground beef or ground fresh turkey
½	cup chopped onion
1	clove garlic, minced
4	teaspoons all-purpose flour
1	tablespoon chili powder
1	15-ounce can Hunt's® Tomato Sauce
½	cup chopped green pepper

8	8- to 10-inch flour tortillas
1	cup shredded mozzarella or cheddar cheese (4 ounces)
	Shredded lettuce (optional)
	Hunt's Ready Tomato Sauces Chunky Salsa (optional)
	Dairy sour cream (optional)

For filling, crumble ground meat into a 2-quart microwave-safe casserole; stir in onion and garlic. Cover; micro-cook on 100% power (high) for 4 to 6 minutes or until meat no longer is pink, stirring once. Drain off fat. Stir in flour and chili powder. Stir in Hunt's Tomato Sauce and green pepper. Cover; cook on high for 5 to 7 minutes or until mixture is thickened and bubbly, stirring twice.

Place *half* of the tortillas between microwave-safe paper towels. Cook on high for 45 to 60 seconds or until softened. Repeat with remaining tortillas.

Spoon about ⅓ *cup* of the filling onto *each* tortilla just below the center. Top *each* with some of the shredded cheese. Fold bottom edge of each tortilla up and over, just to cover the filling. Fold in opposite sides until they meet. Roll up tortilla from bottom. Place *half* of the rolls on a microwave-safe plate. Cover with microwave-safe paper towels. Cook on high for 1 to 2 minutes or until hot. Repeat with remaining rolls. Serve rolls on shredded lettuce and top with Hunt's Ready Tomato Sauces Chunky Salsa and sour cream, if desired.

Nutrition facts per serving: 541 cal., 34 g pro., 51 g carbo., 22 g fat, 80 mg chol., .5 g dietary fiber, 1,152 mg sodium.

Spicy Chicken Tortillas

Makes 4 Servings
Total Time: 20 Minutes

1	pound skinless, boneless chicken breast halves	1	4-ounce can diced green chili peppers, drained
2	teaspoons unsweetened cocoa powder (optional)		Toasted sliced almonds (optional)
1½	teaspoons chili powder	8	flour tortillas, warmed,* or 3 cups hot cooked rice
½	teaspoon ground cumin		Chopped fresh tomato or Hunt's Choice-Cut™ Diced Tomatoes (optional)
½	teaspoon dried oregano, crushed		
¼	teaspoon salt		Shredded lettuce (optional)
1	8-ounce can Hunt's® Tomato Sauce		Sliced avocado (optional)
¼	cup finely chopped onion		
3	cloves garlic, minced		

Rinse chicken; pat dry. Cut chicken into bite-size strips; set aside. Combine cocoa powder, chili powder, cumin, oregano, and salt in a 1½-quart microwave-safe casserole. Stir in Hunt's Tomato Sauce, onion, and garlic. Cover; micro-cook on 100% power (high) for 2 to 3 minutes or until mixture is bubbly around edges, stirring once.

Stir chicken and chili peppers into tomato mixture. Cover; cook on high for 8 to 10 minutes or until chicken is tender and no longer pink, stirring every 3 minutes. Stir in toasted almonds, if desired (see tip on *page 29*). Serve chicken mixture in warm flour tortillas or with hot cooked rice. Top with chopped fresh tomato or Hunt's Choice-Cut Diced Tomatoes, lettuce, and avocado, if desired.

Note: To warm tortillas in the microwave oven, place 4 tortillas between microwave-safe paper towels. Cook on high for 45 to 60 seconds or until softened.

Nutrition facts per serving: 411 cal., 34 g pro., 47 g carbo., 9 g fat, 72 mg chol., 5 g dietary fiber, 1,208 mg sodium.

CHICKEN CACCIATORE

MAKES 6 SERVINGS
TOTAL TIME: 35 MINUTES

½	cup chopped onion		1	bay leaf
2	cloves garlic, minced		2	to 2½ pounds meaty chicken pieces
1	tablespoon Wesson® Oil			(breasts, thighs, drumsticks)
1	cup sliced fresh mushrooms		2	tablespoons cornstarch
1	15-ounce can Hunt's® Tomato Sauce		2	tablespoons cold water
½	cup dry white wine		¾	pound packaged dried fettuccine,
½	cup chicken broth			cooked and drained
1½	to 2 teaspoons dried basil, crushed			

Combine onion, garlic, and Wesson Oil in a 1½-quart microwave-safe casserole. Micro-cook, uncovered, on 100% power (high) about 2 minutes or until onion is tender. Stir in mushrooms, Hunt's Tomato Sauce, wine, broth, basil, bay leaf, ¼ teaspoon *salt,* and ¼ teaspoon *pepper.* Cook, uncovered, on high for 5 to 6 minutes or until boiling, stirring once. Cook, uncovered, on 50% power (medium) for 5 minutes more. Discard bay leaf; set tomato mixture aside.

Skin chicken, if desired. Rinse; pat dry with paper towels. Arrange the chicken pieces, skin side down, in a 2-quart microwave-safe rectangular baking dish with meaty portions toward the edges of the dish. Cover with waxed paper. Cook on high for 12 to 14 minutes or until chicken is tender and no longer pink, turning pieces over and giving dish a half-turn after 6 minutes.

Drain off fat; keep chicken warm. Combine cornstarch and cold water in a small bowl. Stir into tomato mixture. Cook, uncovered, on high for 2 to 4 minutes or until mixture is thickened and bubbly, stirring every minute. Serve over chicken and hot cooked fettuccine.

Nutrition facts per serving: 476 cal., 31 g pro., 51 g carbo.,
15 g fat, 83 mg chol., 3 g dietary fiber, 652 mg sodium.

Pepperoni Super Spuds

MAKES 4 SERVINGS
TOTAL TIME: 25 MINUTES

- 4   medium baking potatoes
- 2   cups Hunt's® Homestyle™ Spaghetti
      Sauce Flavored with Meat*
- 1   7- or 8-ounce can whole kernel corn,
      drained

- 1   4-ounce package sliced pepperoni
- ½   cup shredded mozzarella
      and/or cheddar cheese (2 ounces)

Wash potatoes; pat dry. Prick potatoes several times with a fork; place on a microwave-safe plate. Micro-cook, uncovered, on 100% power (high) for 7 minutes. Rearrange potatoes, using hot pads, so that the part of the potato that faced the outside of the plate now faces the inside. Cook, uncovered, on high for 7 to 10 minutes more or until potatoes are almost tender when pierced with a fork. Let stand for 5 minutes. Use a small knife to cut a deep slit in the top of each potato, from one end of the potato to the other.

Meanwhile, for sauce, stir together Hunt's Homestyle Spaghetti Sauce Flavored with Meat, corn, and pepperoni in a 2-quart microwave-safe casserole. Cook, uncovered, on high for 3 to 5 minutes or until heated through, stirring occasionally. To serve, place each potato on a dinner plate. Ladle some of the sauce on top of each potato. Sprinkle each with cheese.

*Note: Store the leftover spaghetti sauce in a tightly covered plastic container in the refrigerator for up to 1 week.

Nutrition facts per serving: 486 cal., 17 g pro., 69 g carbo., 18 g fat, 34 mg chol., 7 g dietary fiber, 1,362 mg sodium.

SAUCE ON THE SIDE

Leftover Hunt's® Spaghetti Sauce comes in handy as a side dish to perk up any meal. Heat your favorite variety and toss it with cooked pasta. Serve with roast beef or pork, roast chicken or turkey, or poached fish.

CHILI-TOPPED POTATOES

MAKES 4 SERVINGS
TOTAL TIME: 35 MINUTES

4	medium baking potatoes	1½	teaspoons chili powder
¼	cup water	2	cloves garlic, minced
½	pound ground beef	4	cups shredded lettuce
1	small onion, chopped	1	small fresh tomato, chopped, or 1 cup
1	15-ounce can Hunt's® Ready Tomato		Hunt's Choice-Cut™ Diced Tomatoes
	Sauces Chunky Chili	¼	cup sliced green onions
1	8-ounce can red kidney beans, rinsed	½	cup shredded cheddar or American
	and drained		cheese (2 ounces)
1	4-ounce can diced green chili peppers,		
	drained		

Wash potatoes. Cut into ½-inch slices. Place slices in a 2-quart microwave-safe casserole. Add water. Cover; micro-cook on 100% power (high) for 14 to 16 minutes or until tender, stirring once. Drain. Remove potatoes from casserole; keep warm.

Crumble meat into the same casserole; stir in onion. Cover; cook on high for 3 to 4 minutes or until meat no longer is pink and onion is tender, stirring once. Drain off fat. Stir in Hunt's Ready Tomato Sauces Chunky Chili, kidney beans, chili peppers, chili powder, and garlic. Cover; cook on high for 6 to 8 minutes or until heated through, stirring twice.

Arrange *1 cup* of shredded lettuce on *each* of 4 individual plates. Arrange potato slices over the lettuce; spoon the meat mixture on top. Sprinkle with chopped fresh tomato or Hunt's Choice-Cut Diced Tomatoes, green onions, and shredded cheese.

Nutrition facts per serving: 502 cal., 26 g pro., 71 g carbo.,
13 g fat, 57 mg chol., 10 g dietary fiber, 1,170 mg sodium.

FIX-AND-FORGET CROCKERY MEALS

Come home to delicious, ready-to-eat meals, served right from your crockery cooker. To help you save time and effort, each recipe takes advantage of easy-on-the-cook ingredients, including Hunt's® tomato products. From soups and sandwiches to meat and pasta dishes, you'll find plenty of ways to satisfy hungry appetites.

Chunky Vegetable Chili
(see recipe, page 80)

CHUNKY VEGETABLE CHILI

MAKES 4 SERVINGS
PREP TIME: 15 MINUTES • COOK TIME: 8 HOURS

1 medium zucchini, cut into ½-inch pieces (1½ cups)
1 medium green pepper, coarsely chopped
½ cup coarsely chopped onion
½ cup coarsely chopped celery
2 cloves garlic, minced
2 to 3 teaspoons chili powder
1 teaspoon dried oregano, crushed
½ teaspoon ground cumin
2 14½-ounce cans Hunt's® Stewed Tomatoes
1 17-ounce can whole kernel corn
1 15-ounce can black beans, rinsed and drained
1 cup Hunt's Ready Tomato Sauces Chunky Salsa*
Dairy sour cream

Combine zucchini pieces, green pepper, onion, celery, garlic, chili powder, oregano, and cumin in a 3½- or 4-quart crockery cooker. Stir in *undrained* Hunt's Stewed Tomatoes, *undrained* corn, black beans, and Hunt's Ready Tomato Sauces Chunky Salsa.

Cover; cook on low-heat setting for 8 to 10 hours. (Or cook on high-heat setting for 4 to 5 hours.) Serve with sour cream.

*Note: Store the leftover chunky salsa sauce in a tightly covered plastic container in the refrigerator for up to 1 week. See the tips on pages 14, 21, 27, and 66 for ideas on how to use the leftover sauce.

Nutrition facts per serving: 293 cal., 14 g pro., 58 g carbo., 5 g fat, 6 mg chol., 6 g dietary fiber, 1,568 mg sodium.

Note: Pictured on pages 78–79.

Beef and Vegetable Soup

MAKES 6 SERVINGS
PREP TIME: 15 MINUTES • COOK TIME: 8 HOURS

1   **pound ground beef**
½   **cup chopped onion**
2   **cloves garlic, minced**
4   **cups Hunt's® Tomato Juice**
2   **cups pre-shredded coleslaw mix**
1   **14½-ounce can Hunt's Stewed Tomatoes**

1   **10-ounce package frozen whole kernel corn**
1   **9-ounce package frozen cut green beans**
2   **tablespoons Worcestershire sauce**
1   **teaspoon dried basil, crushed**
¼   **teaspoon pepper**
    Corn bread (optional)

Cook ground beef, onion, and garlic in a large skillet until meat is brown. Drain off fat. Combine meat mixture, Hunt's Tomato Juice, coleslaw mix, *undrained* Hunt's Stewed Tomatoes, frozen corn, frozen green beans, Worcestershire sauce, basil, and pepper in a 3½- or 4-quart crockery cooker.

Cover; cook on low-heat setting for 8 to 10 hours. (Or cook on high-heat setting for 4 to 5 hours.) Serve soup with corn bread, if desired.

Nutrition facts per serving: 278 cal., 22 g pro., 26 g carbo., 11 g fat, 56 mg chol., 5 g dietary fiber, 716 mg sodium.

CROCKERY COOKER BASICS

Crockery cookers are not all the same. Before you prepare any of the recipes in this chapter, check to see which type of cooker you own.

These recipes are designed to be used with 3½- to 4-quart crockery cookers with heating coils that wrap around the cooker. This type of cooker provides continuous slow cooking at one temperature. The timings in these recipes won't work for cookers with heating elements that sit below the cooking container and cycle on and off

Italian Bean Soup

MAKES 6 SERVINGS
PREP TIME: 15 MINUTES • STAND TIME: 1 HOUR
COOK TIME: 11½ HOURS

1 cup dry great northern beans	¼ teaspoon pepper
1 cup dry red beans or pinto beans	1 9-ounce package frozen Italian-style green beans or cut green beans
1 28-ounce can Hunt's® Whole Tomatoes, cut up	1 tablespoon margarine or butter
1 medium onion, chopped	⅛ teaspoon garlic salt
2 tablespoons instant beef bouillon granules	⅛ teaspoon dried Italian seasoning, crushed
2 cloves garlic, minced	12 ½-inch-thick slices baguette-style French bread or six 1-inch-thick slices Italian bread
2 teaspoons dried Italian seasoning, crushed	

Rinse both types of dry beans. Combine rinsed beans and 5 cups *cold water* in Dutch oven. Bring to boiling; reduce heat. Simmer for 2 minutes; remove from heat. Cover; let stand for 1 hour. (Or soak rinsed beans overnight in a covered pan.) Drain and rinse beans.

Combine the soaked beans, 4 cups fresh *water*, the *undrained* Hunt's Whole Tomatoes (cut up), onion, bouillon, garlic, the 2 teaspoons Italian seasoning, and pepper in a 3½- or 4-quart crockery cooker. Cover; cook on low-heat setting for 11 to 13 hours or until beans are almost tender. (Or cook on high-heat setting for 5½ to 6½ hours.) Run frozen green beans under cold running water to separate; stir into soup in cooker. Cover; cook for 30 minutes more on high-heat setting.

Meanwhile, for herb toast, stir together margarine, garlic salt, and the ⅛ teaspoon Italian seasoning. Spread some of the margarine mixture on 1 side of *each* bread slice. Place bread, margarine side up, on the unheated rack of a broiler pan. Broil 4 to 5 inches from the heat for 45 to 60 seconds or until crisp and light brown.

To serve, float 2 small pieces or 1 large piece of herb toast on top of each bowl of soup. Serve immediately.

Nutrition facts per serving: 451 cal., 21 g pro., 81 g carbo., 5 g fat, 0 mg chol., 18 g dietary fiber, 1,774 mg sodium.

EASY ITALIAN CHICKEN BREASTS

MAKES 4 SERVINGS
PREP TIME: 15 MINUTES • COOK TIME: 5 HOURS

¾ pound skinless, boneless chicken breast halves
1 9-ounce package frozen Italian-style green beans
1 cup fresh mushrooms, quartered
1 small onion, sliced ¼ inch thick
1 14½-ounce can Hunt's® Stewed Tomatoes

1 6-ounce can Hunt's Tomato Paste
1 teaspoon dried Italian seasoning, crushed
2 cloves garlic, minced
½ pound packaged dried fettuccine, cooked and drained

Rinse chicken; pat dry. Cut chicken into 1-inch pieces.

Combine green beans, mushrooms, and onion in a 3½- or 4-quart crockery cooker. Place chicken on top of vegetables. Combine *undrained* Hunt's Stewed Tomatoes, Hunt's Tomato Paste, Italian seasoning, and garlic. Pour over chicken.

Cover; cook on low-heat setting for 5 to 6 hours. (Or cook on high-heat setting for 2½ to 3 hours.) Serve over hot cooked fettuccine.

Nutrition facts per serving: 412 cal., 42 g pro., 61 g carbo.,
4 g fat, 66 mg chol., 6 g dietary fiber, 470 mg sodium.

QUICK-COOKING STRATEGIES

To make meal preparation extra easy, buy ingredients in the form needed for a recipe. Here are some options:
- Shredded cheese
- Cut-up chicken
- Boned and skinned chicken breasts
- Cut-up meats, such as stew meat
- Sliced pepperoni
- Bread crumbs

- Dried minced onion
- Diced chili peppers
- Torn mixed greens
- Salad ingredients from a salad bar
- Quick-cooking rice
- Bottled minced garlic
- Hunt's® Ready Tomato Sauces
- Hunt's Choice-Cut™ Diced Tomatoes

Spicy Ginger-and-Tomato Chicken

MAKES 6 SERVINGS
PREP TIME: 25 MINUTES • COOK TIME: 6 HOURS

1	2½- to 3-pound cut up broiler-fryer chicken, skinned	1	tablespoon snipped fresh cilantro or parsley
1	14½-ounce can Hunt's® Choice-Cut™ Diced Tomatoes	4	cloves garlic, minced
1	8-ounce can Hunt's Tomato Sauce	2	teaspoons brown sugar
2	tablespoons quick-cooking tapioca	½	to 1 teaspoon crushed red pepper
1	tablespoon grated gingerroot	3	cups hot cooked couscous or rice

Rinse chicken pieces; pat dry with paper towels. Place skinned chicken pieces in a 3½- or 4-quart crockery cooker.

Combine *undrained* Hunt's Choice-Cut Diced Tomatoes, Hunt's Tomato Sauce, tapioca, gingerroot, cilantro or parsley, garlic, brown sugar, and crushed red pepper in a medium bowl. Pour over chicken.

Cover; cook on low-heat setting for 6 to 7 hours. (Or cook on high-heat setting for 3 to 3½ hours.) Skim off fat. Serve with hot cooked couscous or rice.

Nutrition facts per serving: 270 cal., 25 g pro., 30 g carbo., 5 g fat, 63 mg chol., 4 g dietary fiber, 436 mg sodium.

Italian-Sausage Heros

MAKES 8 SERVINGS
PREP TIME: 20 MINUTES • COOK TIME: 10 HOURS

1 pound bulk Italian sausage	4 teaspoons quick-cooking tapioca
½ pound ground beef	1 teaspoon sugar
1 cup chopped onion	1 teaspoon dried oregano, crushed
1 15-ounce can Hunt's® Ready Tomato Sauces Original Italian	⅛ teaspoon pepper
	Dash garlic powder
1 8-ounce can Hunt's Tomato Sauce	½ cup sliced pitted ripe olives
1 4-ounce can mushroom stems and pieces, drained	8 French-style rolls, split lengthwise
	6 slices mozzarella cheese (6 ounces)

Cook sausage, ground beef, and onion in a large skillet until meat is brown and onion is tender. Drain off fat. Pat with paper towels to remove excess fat.

Combine Hunt's Ready Tomato Sauces Original Italian, Hunt's Tomato Sauce, mushrooms, tapioca, sugar, oregano, pepper, and garlic powder in a 3½- or 4-quart crockery cooker. Stir in meat mixture.

Cover; cook on low-heat setting for 10 to 12 hours. (Or cook on high-heat setting for 4 to 5 hours.) Stir in olives just before serving.

To serve, use a fork to hollow out bottom halves of rolls, leaving ¼-inch-thick shells. (Reserve bread pieces for another use.) Cut cheese slices into thin strips. Place some of the cheese strips in bottom halves of rolls. Spoon meat mixture into rolls. Place remaining cheese strips on top of meat mixture. Cover with bun tops. Serve immediately.

Nutrition facts per serving: 467 cal., 27 g pro., 40 g carbo., 22 g fat, 67 mg chol., 3 g dietary fiber, 1,353 mg sodium.

POT ROAST WITH NOODLES

MAKES 8 SERVINGS
PREP TIME: 30 MINUTES • COOK TIME: 10 HOURS

1 2- to 2½-pound beef chuck pot roast	1 6-ounce can Hunt's Tomato Paste
1 tablespoon Wesson® Oil	1 tablespoon brown sugar
2 medium carrots, coarsely chopped	½ teaspoon salt
2 stalks celery, sliced	¼ teaspoon pepper
1 medium onion, sliced	1 bay leaf
2 cloves garlic, minced	1 pound packaged dried noodles,
1 tablespoon quick-cooking tapioca	cooked and drained
1 14½-ounce can Hunt's® Stewed Tomatoes	

Trim fat from pot roast. If necessary, cut roast to fit into crockery cooker. Heat Wesson Oil in a large skillet. Cook pot roast on all sides in hot oil until brown.

Meanwhile, combine carrots, celery, onion, and garlic in a 3½- or 4-quart crockery cooker. Sprinkle tapioca over vegetables. Place meat on top of vegetables.

Combine *undrained* Hunt's Stewed Tomatoes, Hunt's Tomato Paste, brown sugar, salt, pepper, and bay leaf in a small bowl. Pour over the meat.

Cover; cook on low-heat setting for 10 to 12 hours. (Or cook on high-heat setting for 4 to 5 hours.) Discard bay leaf. Skim off fat. Serve with hot cooked noodles.

Nutrition facts per serving: 458 cal., 41 g pro., 58 g carbo.,
11 g fat, 169 mg chol., 2 g dietary fiber, 430 mg sodium.

ITALIAN STEAK ROLLS

MAKES 6 SERVINGS
PREP TIME: 40 MINUTES • COOK TIME: 7 HOURS

1½	to 2 pounds boneless beef round steak	1	clove garlic, minced
½	cup grated carrot	¼	teaspoon black pepper
⅓	cup chopped zucchini	1	tablespoon Wesson® Oil
⅓	cup chopped red or green sweet pepper	1¾	cups Hunt's® Chunky Spaghetti Sauce Marinara*
¼	cup sliced green onions	¾	pound packaged dried pasta, cooked and drained
2	tablespoons grated Parmesan cheese		
1	tablespoon snipped parsley		

Trim fat from meat. Cut meat into 6 portions. Place the meat between 2 pieces of clear plastic wrap and, with a meat mallet, pound each piece to an ⅛- to ¼-inch thickness.

For filling, combine next 8 ingredients. Spoon *one-sixth* of the filling onto *each* piece of meat. Roll up meat around the filling; tie each roll with string or secure with wooden toothpicks. Heat Wesson Oil in a large skillet. Cook meat rolls in hot oil until brown on all sides. Transfer meat rolls to a 3½- or 4-quart crockery cooker. Pour Hunt's Chunky Spaghetti Sauce Marinara over the meat rolls.

Cover; cook on low-heat setting for 7 to 8 hours. (Or cook on high-heat setting for 3½ to 4 hours.) Skim off fat. Discard string or toothpicks. Serve meat rolls with hot cooked pasta.

Note: Store the leftover spaghetti sauce in a tightly covered plastic container in the refrigerator for up to 1 week.

Nutrition facts per serving: 448 cal., 33 g pro., 53 g carbo., 12 g fat, 74 mg chol., 1 g dietary fiber, 390 mg sodium.

DIPPERS' DELIGHT

Heat leftover Hunt's® Spaghetti Sauce and serve it as a dip for snacks. It's delicious with prepared frozen pizza rolls, warm soft pretzels, bread sticks, or even wontons.

BEEF-VEGETABLE STEW

MAKES 6 SERVINGS
PREP TIME: 25 MINUTES • COOK TIME: 8½ HOURS

1½ pounds boneless beef top round steak,
   cut 1 inch thick
   Wesson® No Stick Cooking Spray
1 11-ounce can condensed cheddar
   cheese soup
¼ cup dried minced onion
3 tablespoons Hunt's® Tomato Paste
½ teaspoon lemon-pepper seasoning

2 cups small whole fresh mushrooms,
   halved
1 9-ounce package frozen Italian-style
   green beans
½ cup buttermilk
¾ pound packaged dried fettuccine,
   cooked and drained

Trim fat from beef. Cut meat into 1-inch pieces. Spray a *cold* 4-quart Dutch oven with Wesson No Stick Cooking Spray. Preheat over medium heat. Cook meat, *half* at a time, in hot Dutch oven until brown, stirring occasionally.

Place meat in a 3½- or 4-quart crockery cooker. Combine condensed soup, dried minced onion, Hunt's Tomato Paste, and lemon-pepper seasoning. Pour over the meat. Add mushrooms. Cover; cook on low-heat setting for 8 to 10 hours. (Or cook on high-heat setting for 4 to 5 hours.)

Run frozen green beans under cold running water to separate; add to crockery cooker. Stir in buttermilk. Cover; cook on high-heat setting for 30 minutes more. Serve stew over hot cooked fettuccine.

Nutrition facts per serving: 469 cal., 38 g pro., 54 g carbo.,
11 g fat, 84 mg chol., 3 g dietary fiber, 558 mg sodium.

TOMATO PASTE ON CALL

When a recipe calls for a partial can of Hunt's® Tomato Paste, divide the remainder into 1- or 2-tablespoon portions and freeze in freezer bags. Pull out one or two of the frozen portions the next time a recipe calls for a tablespoon or two of tomato paste. Or for extra flavor, add a portion when you make vegetable soup or sauces.

Beef and Vegetables in Tomato Sauce

Makes 6 to 8 Servings
Prep Time: 25 Minutes • Cook Time: 8 Hours

1½ pounds boneless beef bottom round steak
1   tablespoon Wesson® Oil
2   medium carrots, cut into ½-inch pieces
2   stalks celery, cut into ½-inch pieces
1   cup quartered fresh mushrooms
½   cup sliced green onions
3   tablespoons quick-cooking tapioca
1   14½-ounce can Hunt's® Stewed Tomatoes

1   cup beef broth
½   cup dry red wine, white wine, or beef broth
1   teaspoon dried Italian seasoning, crushed
½   teaspoon salt
¼   teaspoon pepper
1   bay leaf
¾   to 1 pound packaged dried noodles, cooked and drained

Trim fat from meat; cut meat into 1-inch cubes. Heat Wesson Oil in a large skillet. Cook meat, *half* at a time, in hot oil until brown, stirring occasionally. Drain off fat.

Transfer meat to a 3½- or 4-quart crockery cooker. Add carrots, celery, mushrooms, and green onions. Sprinkle with quick-cooking tapioca.

Combine *undrained* Hunt's Stewed Tomatoes, the 1 cup beef broth, the wine or broth, Italian seasoning, salt, pepper, and bay leaf. Pour over vegetables and meat.

Cover; cook on low-heat setting for 8 to 10 hours. (Or cook on high-heat setting for 4 to 5 hours.) Discard bay leaf. Skim off fat. Serve over hot cooked noodles.

Nutrition facts per serving: 471 cal., 33 g pro., 51 g carbo., 13 g fat, 163 mg chol., 5 g dietary fiber, 561 mg sodium.

Pasta with Mushroom-Tomato Sauce

MAKES 6 SERVINGS
PREP TIME: 15 MINUTES • COOK TIME: 8 HOURS

2	14½-ounce cans Hunt's® Choice-Cut™ Diced Tomatoes
2	cups sliced fresh mushrooms
1	6-ounce can Hunt's Tomato Paste
½	cup chopped onion
2	cloves garlic, minced
2	tablespoons grated Parmesan cheese
2	teaspoons dried oregano, crushed
2	teaspoons brown sugar

1½	teaspoons dried basil, crushed
½	teaspoon salt
½	teaspoon fennel seed, crushed (optional)
¼	to ½ teaspoon crushed red pepper
1	bay leaf
¾	pound packaged dried spaghetti, linguine, or other pasta, cooked and drained
	Grated Parmesan cheese (optional)

Combine *undrained* Hunt's Choice-Cut Diced Tomatoes, mushrooms, Hunt's Tomato Paste, onion, garlic, the 2 tablespoons Parmesan cheese, oregano, brown sugar, basil, salt, fennel seed (if desired), crushed red pepper, and bay leaf in a 3½- or 4-quart crockery cooker.

Cover; cook on low-heat setting for 8 to 10 hours. (Or cook on high-heat setting for 4 to 5 hours.)

Discard bay leaf. Serve sauce over hot cooked pasta. Top with additional grated Parmesan cheese, if desired.

Nutrition facts per serving: 283 cal., 19 g pro., 56 g carbo., 2 g fat, 2 mg chol., 3 g dietary fiber, 608 mg sodium.

RECIPE INDEX

TIPS

NUTRITION FIGURES

Each recipe in this book lists the nutrition facts for one serving. Here's how these values were calculated. When a recipe gives a choice of ingredients (such as ground beef or ground fresh turkey), the first choice was used for the analysis. If an ingredient is listed as optional in a recipe, it was not included in the analysis. All values were rounded to the nearest whole number.

RECIPES-BY-PRODUCT INDEX

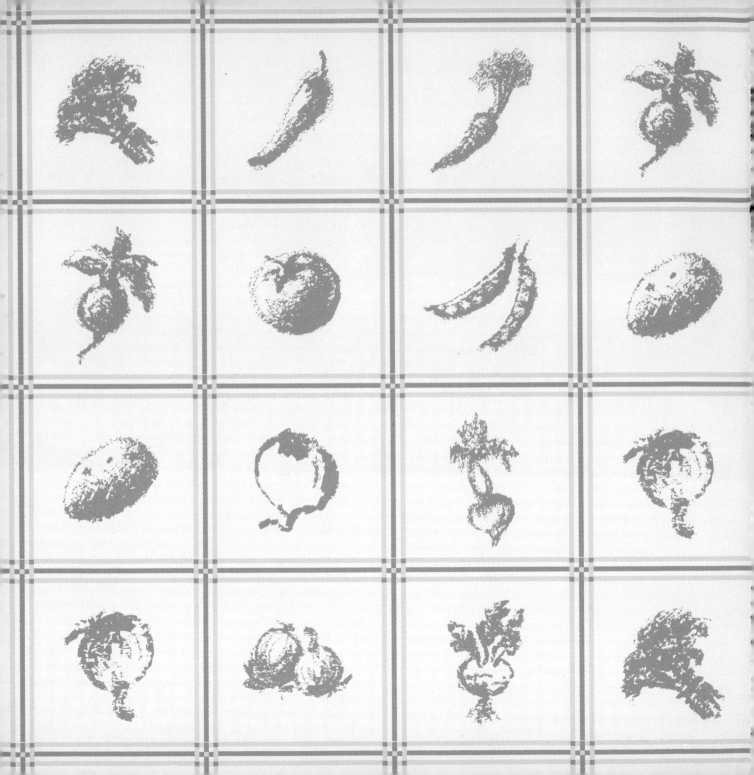